Cape May Fare

A recipe collection from friends and members of
Mid-Atlantic Center for the Arts

Published by
Mid-Atlantic Center for the Arts
P.O. Box 340
Cape May, New Jersey 08204
1987

Copies of CAPE MAY FARE may be obtained from
Cape May Fare
Mid-Atlantic Center for the Arts
P.O. Box 340
Cape May, New Jersey 08204

ISBN # 0-9663295-1-1

Library of Congress Catalog Card Number
87-061236

First Printing	1987	5,000 copies
Second Printing	1991	1,000 copies
Third Printing	1993	1,000 copies
Fourth Printing	1995	1,000 copies
Fifth Printing	1997	2,000 copies
Sixth Printing	1998	3,000 copies

Printed in the USA by

WIMMER
The Wimmer Companies
Memphis
1-800-548-2537

ALL ABOUT MAC
(Mid-Atlantic Center for the Arts)

Since its founding in 1970, the Mid-Atlantic Center for the Arts (MAC) has played a leading role in spurring Cape May's revival as one of the country's premier seashore resorts—through its promotion of the area's Victorian architecture, its year-round schedule of special events and its sponsorship of the performing arts.

A not-for-profit organization with over 1,100 members, MAC was established to save from the wrecker's ball one of Cape May's proudest landmarks, the Emlen Physick Estate. Over the past decade, MAC volunteers have poured thousands of hours of labor into the restoration of this Frank Furness-designed masterpiece of 1879. As a result, what was once an overgrown, gutted derelict has been transformed into one of Cape May's leading attractions—a top quality Victorian house museum whose well-maintained grounds host a wide range of community and cultural events. While much has been accomplished, every year has seen continued efforts to bring the Estate to still higher levels of perfection. Thus the on-going restoration of the Physick Estate remains a major focus of MAC's fund raising activities. It was with this need in mind that the cookbook concept came into being. With the proceeds from the sale of Cape May Fare, we hope to restore the grounds and gardens to their Victorian splendor, thus continuing the revival of this spectacular property.

B. Michael Zuckerman, Director

ABOUT OUR COVER

Emlen Physick Estate (front cover)
The centerpiece of the Emlen Physick Estate is the 18-room mansion designed by renowned architect Frank Furness. Built in 1879 in the Stick Style, it has been painstakingly restored as a high-quality Victorian house museum by the Mid-Atlantic Center for the Arts. Its interior contains outstanding examples of Eastlake-style furnishings and fixtures (many of which were original family pieces designed by Furness, himself), as well as collections of costumes, toys and artifacts. For tour information, call (609) 884-5404.

Cape May Point Lighthouse (rear cover)

Built in 1859, the Cape May Point Lighthouse is located at the southern-most tip of the New Jersey shore (at the mouth of Delaware Bay). It originally contained a 1st order lens that sat 167 feet above sea level, and its beacon is still operated today by the U.S. Coast Guard as an aid to navigation. In December 1986, the Lighthouse was leased to the Mid-Atlantic Center for the Arts with the goals of restoring it and opening it to the public as a Lighthouse Museum. For further information, call (609) 884-5404.

The Mid-Atlantic Center of the Arts
Cookbook Committee

Chairman   Rona Craig

Karen Andrus
K.C. Bennett
Katie Gregg
Florence Heal
Christy Igoe
Sally Brice-O'Hara
Ann Miller

Sally Sachs
Charlotte Todd
Ann Tourison
Mary Trexler
Pat Trumbull
Joan Warner

Artist
Jon David Hallberg

Typists

Mary Trexler   Joan Alvarez

To the many friends and members of MAC who shared their valued recipes with us, the Cookbook Committee expresses our sincere thanks. We regret that every recipe could not be used because of similarity and lack of space. We are truly grateful for all the treasured recipes from our contributors.

TABLE OF CONTENTS

Appetizers and Beverages 7

Soups, Salads and Sandwiches 33

Cheese, Eggs and Pasta.. 59

Bread 75

Entrees

    Seafood 89

    Poultry 105

    Meat 124

Vegetables and Grains...139

Accompaniments...163

Sweets

    Pies 181

    Cakes 191

    Cookies 207

    Candy 213

    Desserts 214

    Index 223

Appetizers
and
Beverages

-JDW-1987

Dr. Henry Hunt House, 1881
209 Congress Place

Built on land that, at one time, was part of Congress Hall's backyard, this house is a study in Queen Anne styling. Beautifully turned wood columns, the whimsical roof-top gazebo and the lovely stained glass create a very enchanting appearance.

ARTICHOKE HEARTS

1 jar or can artichoke hearts
1 cup Parmesan cheese

1 cup mayonnaise
½ cup sour cream

Mix altogether. Put in oven until bubbly at 350 degrees for 20 to 25 minutes. Serve with crackers. Yields 8 to 10 servings.

Ann Tourison

CHRISTMAS CHEESE BALL

2 (8-ounce) packages cream
   cheese
1 (8½-ounce) can crushed
   pineapple
2 cups chopped pecans, divided
¼ cup chopped green pepper

2 tablespoons chopped onion
1 teaspoon salt
Dash of hot pepper sauce
Maraschino cherries

Soften cream cheese, add well-drained pineapple, mix well. Add 1 cup pecans, pepper, onion, salt and pepper sauce. Mix well. Refrigerate until hardened, form into two balls, roll in 1 cup pecans, garnish with pineapple, maraschino cherries and chopped parsley. Yields 2 cheese balls.

Mary Suzanne Roehm
Gross Pointe Woods, Michigan

BACON WRAPPED CHICKEN LIVERS

1 pound chicken livers

1 pound bacon

Cut chicken livers in half. Cut the bacon strips in half. Wrap bacon around chicken livers and secure with toothpicks. Place in a baking pan. Broil until brown and crisp. Drain on paper towels. Serves 6. *Easy, great for last minute dinner or as a pass around at parties.*

Christy Igoe
Seaville, New Jersey

BARBARA GORDON'S CHEESE APPETIZER

2 packages plain Wispride®
    cheese
Scallions
1 (8-ounce) package cream cheese

Dash of sherry
Dash of Worcestershire sauce

Whole jar of Rafferty's chut-nut or Major Gray's regular chutney. Soften and mix cheese. Add sherry and Worcestershire. Pack into crock (can be done ahead of time). Top with chutney. Chop scallions on top. May be topped with preserves. Serve with crackers - cut through all layers. Serves 6 to 8. *Always a big hit!*

Jan Wood, Woodleigh House

ARTICHOKE NIBBLES

2 (6-ounce) jars marinated
    artichoke hearts
1 small onion, finely chopped
1 clove garlic, minced
4 eggs
¼ cup fine dry bread crumbs

⅛ teaspoon pepper
½ teaspoon oregano
½ pound sharp Cheddar cheese,
    shredded (2 cups)
2 tablespoons minced parsley

Drain marinade from 1 jar of artichokes into a frying pan. Drain the other jar. Chop all artichoke and set aside. Add onion, garlic to frying pan. Saute until onion is limp. In a bowl beat the eggs with a fork. Add the crumbs, pepper and oregano. Stir in the cheese, parsley, artichokes, and onion mixture. Turn into a greased bake pan. Bake at 325 degrees for 30 minutes or until set. Let set in pan then cut 1-inch squares. Serve hot or cold. Can be made ahead. *This is great for passing hot or cold. Hot as a great company vegetable*. Yields 10 to 18 servings. *Note:* Can be made with chopped spinach instead of artichokes.

Ann Tourison

10

DELICIOUS CHEESE RING

1 small onion, grated finely
1 cup mayonnaise
1 cup finely chopped nuts
1 pound sharp cheese, grated

Dash of black and cayenne pepper
Optional: Strawberry or other
    preserves

Combine all ingredients, except preserves. Season with pepper. Mix well and place in lightly greased 5 or 6 cup ring mold. Refrigerate for several hours or overnight. Serve with crackers and if desired, fill center with preserves, or serve plain with drinks. Yields 1 ring.

Elizabeth Von Schlichten

HOLIDAY CHEESE BALLS

1 pound mild cheese, grated
1 pound sharp New York
    Cheddar cheese, grated
1 (8-ounce) carton cottage cheese
1 (3-ounce) package bleu cheese
1 (8-ounce) cream cheese
1 ounce Roquefort cheese

1 cup chopped nuts
2 cloves garlic, grated
1 tablespoon Worcestershire
    sauce
1 teaspoon hot pepper sauce
½ cup whipped margarine

Mix all ingredients in large bowl. Shape into size balls desired, roll in flour to give smooth appearance. Sprinkle with paprika and parsley leaves. Yields 2 large or 3 medium-sized cheese balls.

Mary Suzanne Roehm
Grosse Pointe Woods, Michigan

CHEESE COOKIES

2 cups flour
1 cup butter
8 ounces grated Cheddar cheese

½ teaspoon red pepper
½ teaspoon salt
2 cups crispy rice cereal

Mix ingredients. Heat oven to 350 degrees. Drop cookies on cookie sheet by teaspoonfuls. Bake 15 minutes. Serves 8.

Marjorie Ward

11

GLAZED CHICKEN WINGS

3 to 4 pounds chicken wings, cut in half

Salt to taste
Garlic powder to taste

Arrange seasoned wings in single layer in large pan. Bake at 350 degrees for 35 to 40 minutes.

Glaze

1 (10-ounce) jar pineapple preserves

1 (10-ounce) jar apricot preserves
Juice of 1 lemon

Mix preserves and lemon. Dip wing into mixture. Coat well. Place in clean pan in single layer. Bake at 450 degrees for 15 to 20 minutes, until well glazed. To freeze, don't glaze as long. Cool 1 hour before freezing. Reheat at 350 degrees then turn oven to 450 degrees for 5 minutes. Serves 6 to 8. *Enjoy!*

Anita de Satnick

CHICKEN NUGGETS

4 whole chicken breasts
½ cup unseasoned fine dry bread crumbs
¼ cup grated Parmesan cheese

½ teaspoon thyme leaves
1 teaspoon basil leaves
¼ cup melted butter

Bone and skin chicken, cut into nuggets 1¼-inch square. Combine dry ingredients. Dip chicken pieces into butter and then into crumb mix. Place in single layer on foil lined baking sheet. Bake until golden brown at 400 degrees for 10 to 15 minutes. Serves 60.

CHICKEN STICKS

3 pounds chicken wings
¾ cup melted butter
1½ cups flour
⅓ cup sesame seed

1 tablespoon salt
½ teaspoon ginger
Juice of ½ lemon

Cut the chicken wings in three sections and discard the wing tips. Dip remaining sections in butter. Mix the flour, sesame seed, salt and ginger and roll chicken section in mixture. Place in a foil-lined baking dish. Bake at 350 degrees for 1 hour, then sprinkle with lemon juice. Serves 6 to 8.

CHICKEN SALAD BALLS

1 cup cooked chicken
1 tablespoon chopped onions
2 tablespoons chopped pimiento

Dash hot sauce
½ cup mayonnaise
1 cup chopped pecans

Combine all ingredients, mixing well. Chill several hours, shape into 1-inch balls. Yields 2 to 2½ dozen.

Nan Danner

CHILI CON QUESCO DIP

1 (16-ounce) package pasteurized
  processed cheese, cubed

1 (7 to 8-ounce) can Acapulco dip
  or jalapeno relish

Melt together in microwave until melted. Stir occasionally. Serve with tortilla strips. (Doritos®). Serves 6 to 8.

Lynda Leaming

CHILI-CHEESE PINWHEELS

1 (package) dozen flour tortillas, medium or small size
1 (8-ounce) package cream cheese, softened
1 (4-ounce) can chopped green chilies, drained
2 tablespoons (or more to taste) taco sauce, chunky style or green chili salsa
1 teaspoon (or more) chili powder
½ teaspoon garlic powder
1 tablespoon (or more) taco seasonings
Dash of hot pepper sauce
3 to 4 tablespoons chopped black olives

Hand blend all ingredients and spread on the flour tortillas. Roll up and refrigerate 1 hour or more until firm. Slice in ½ to 1 inch pinewheels. Yields 8 to 10 servings.

Lynda Leaming
Orange, California

CHILI DIP

1 (8-ounce) package cream cheese, cubed
2 (15-ounce) cans chili, 1 with beans, 1 without
½ to 1 teaspoon hot pepper sauce or more, to taste
½ teaspoon garlic powder

Melt butter, stirring every 2 minutes on High in microwave until hot and bubbly. Serve with tortilla chips (plain Doritos®). Yields 3 cups.

Lynda Leaming
Orange, California

CLAM PIE

2 (8-ounce) can minced clams
2 tablespoons lemon juice
1 medium onion chopped
4 sprigs parsley
½ cup butter or margarine

1 teaspoon oregano
¼ teaspoon pepper
¾ cup Italian bread crumbs
American cheese in strips

Slowly simmer clams with clam juice and lemon juice. Add rest of ingredients. Mix. Place in 8-inch pie plate. Cut American cheese in strips and lattice. Bake in 350 degree oven until hot and cheese melts (about 10 minutes). Serves 10 as a dip. Serve with Triscuits or other crisp crackers as an hors d'oeuvre.

Jessie Lisk
Springfield, Pennsylvania

CORN CRISPS (AKA HOMEMADE FRITOS)

1½ cup yellow cornmeal
3 tablespoons unsalted butter

½ teaspoon salt (or to taste)
1 cup boiling water

Preheat oven to 350. Put first three ingredients into bowl. Pour in boiling water. Mix. Let sit for five minutes. Spoon onto ungreased cookie sheets into 12 to 20 mounds. Flatten with a spoon. They will be uneven and mushy-that's right. Bake 30 to 35 minutes or until lightly browned on the edges. Serve immediately or that day. *That is perfect with guacamole. Dunk them in while they are still hot. This can serve 2 to 6, but I have been known to eat them all myself!*

Louisa Hull, Louisa's

CRAB CANAPES

1 can crabmeat
6 English muffins
½ cup margarine

1½ teaspoon mayonnaise
½ teaspoon garlic salt
½ teaspoon seasoning salt

Mash all ingredients except muffins together. Spread on split English muffins. Freeze 15 minutes. Cut into eighths. Can be returned to freezer in plastic bags. Broil until brown and bubbly. Serves 12.

Juile Merson

CRAB MEAT PUFFS

6 English muffins
½ cup margarine softened
2 tablespoons mayonnaise
½ teaspoon seasoned salt
¼ teaspoon garlic salt

1 (6½ to 7-ounce) can crabmeat, drained
1 (5-ounce) jar Old English sharp Cheddar cheese

Slice each English muffin in half. Put remaining ingredients in small mixer bowl; mix well. Spread on English muffin halves; cut halves into quarters (e.g., each whole English muffin makes 8 canapes). You may freeze them now until ready for use. (They may be kept frozen for weeks). Either broil until they puff up and are bubbly and slightly golden brown or bake 15 minutes at 350 degrees. Serve hot. *Note:* Pick over crab carefully for pieces of bone and shell. Yields 48 pieces.

Mary Ellen McCaffrey Colella

CRAB SPREAD

1 (8-ounce) package cream cheese
1 teaspoon garlic powder
1 teaspoon lemon juice
1 teaspoon Worcestershire sauce

¼ cup mayonnaise
1 can crabmeat
1 jar chili sauce

Mix cream cheese, garlic, lemon juice and Worcestershire and mayonnaise mix with beater. Put in dish. Put crab meat on top with 1 jar chili sauce. Serve with crackers. Serves 6 to 10. *Good.*

Maria Quaglio
Haddonfield, New Jersey

CURRY DIP

2 cups mayonnaise
3 tablespoons each: honey, catsup and grated onion

1 tablespoon curry
Salt and pepper
6 drops hot pepper sauce

Mix all together and refrigerate until ready to use. Serve with raw vegetables. Yields about 2 cups.

Martha Brown
Bluebell, Pennsylvania

CURRY PATE

2 (3-ounce) packages cream
  cheese softened
1 cup shredded sharp Cheddar
  cheese
2 tablespoons dry sherry wine

½ teaspoon curry powder
¼ teaspoon salt
1 (8-ounce) jar mango chutney,
  finely chopped
⅓ cup finely sliced green onions

Beat together thoroughly the cream cheese, Cheddar cheese, sherry, curry powder and salt. Spread on serving platter-shaping a layer ½-inch thick. Chill until firm. At serving time spread with chopped chutney and sprinkle with green onions. Serve on bread wafers. Serves 8. *An easy hors d'ouerve to carry to a party-take a small cheese spatula for serving and crackers! Found in Mt. Lebanon News (Pittsburgh).*

Margaret R. Goodwin
Avalon, New Jersey

DILL'N ONION DIP

⅔ cup mayonnaise
⅔ cup dairy sour cream
1 tablespoon green onions,
 · shredded

1 tablespoon parsley
1 teaspoon dill weed
1 teaspoon seasoned salt

Mix and chill. Good with potato chips, corn chips, or crisp raw vegetables. Yield: 1½ to 2 cups.

Virginia Soller
Arlington, Virginia

MARIMBA DIP

½ pound pasteurized processed
  cheese
2 tablespoon mayonnaise
1 (4½-ounce) can deviled ham

1 tablespoon finely chopped onion
¼ teaspoon hot pepper sauce
3 tablespoons tomato juice

Melt cheese over low heat. Stir in mayonnaise, deviled ham, onion and pepper sauce until well blended. Gradually stir in tomato juice mixing very well. If dip seems too thick, add more juice. Serve with vegetables, breadsticks, etc. Yields about 2 cups.

Kay Keetley
Gloucester, New Jersey

17

MEAT BALL APPETIZERS

1 pound ground beef
½ cup bread crumbs
½ teaspoon oregano
½ teaspoon salt

¼ cup milk
1 egg, beaten
Favorite pie crust recipe

Preheat oven to 375 degrees. Combine all ingredients, except pastry. Shape into 32 small meat balls. Prepare pastry. Roll to form two 12-inch squares. Cut into sixteen 3-inch squares. Place uncooked meatball in center. Bring opposite corners together and pinch to seal. Brush with egg. Bake on ungreased cookie sheet about 15 minutes. Yields about 2½ dozen.

Mary H. Raymond

PARTY MEATBALLS

Meat Mixture
2½ cups ground beef
8 drops hot sauce
1 egg
2 teaspoons soy sauce

⅔ cup crumbs
2 cloves garlic
½ teaspoon oregano or thyme

Serving Sauce
1 cup beef stock
1 teaspoon soy sauce
2 tablespoons tomato sauce

2 tablespoons Dijon mustard
  beaten with
¼ cup dry white wine

Mix all mixture ingredients. Roll into 1-inch balls. Bake at 450 degrees for 8 minutes to brown. Drain. Set aside. Serving sauce: Simmer sauce ingredients about 5 minutes. Keep warm. Add meat balls. To serve, place in warming dish. Yields about 3 to 3½ dozen. *Everyone loves these. I use this recipe for my Holiday Buffet every year.*

Mildred Warmuz
Towanda, New York

STUFFED MUSHROOMS

20 large mushrooms
1 pound roll package breakfast
  sausage (mild or hot)

1 pint sour cream
Seasoned bread crumbs

Wash mushrooms and carefully remove stems. Cook sausage thoroughly and drain completely of all grease (squeeze sausage in paper towels several times). Mix sausage and sour cream together. Add bread crumbs until the mixture holds together well. Fill mushroom caps on flat baking sheet then bake at 400 degrees for 15 minutes. Serves 10 to 15. The stuffing mixture holds together well. Fill mushroom caps on flat baking sheet then bake at 400 degrees for 15 minutes. Serves 10 to 15.

Margaret Ryan

HOT MUSHROOM HORS D'OEUVRES

1 large onion, finely chopped
1 teaspoon butter
¾ pounds mushroons, chopped
Salt and pepper, to taste
¾ pound cream cheese, softened

½ teaspoon Worcestershire
¼ teaspoon MSG powder
1½ pounds white bread
½ to 1 cup melted butter

Saute onion in 1 teaspoon butter; add mushrooms for 2 minutes. Season with salt and pepper, stir in cream cheese, Worcestershire sauce, garlic powder and MSG. Remove from heat. Remove crusts from bread slices and flatten with rolling pin. Spread the cooled cream cheese mixture on thickly and roll in jelly-roll fashion. Fasten with toothpicks and chill briefly to set mixture and facilitate slicing. Preheat broiler while slicing rolls. Slice into ¼-inch thickness and place flat on cookie sheet. Brush liberally with melted butter and run under broiler until golden. Serve at once. Serves 10 to 12. *May be frozen indefinitely in a plastic bag, either sliced or left in rolls. Just butter and broil as needed.*

Cindy Schmucker, The Bedford

PICKLED MUSHROOMS

Approximately 2 pounds fresh
mushrooms
Salad oil (1 cup per jar)
Vinegar (1 cup per jar)
Garlic (1 clove per jar)

Dried parsley (1 generous pinch)
flakes
Oregano (1 generous pinch)
Salt (1 teaspoon per jar)
Freshly ground pepper to taste

Wash and clean fresh mushrooms using a porcelain (or stainless steel) pan.
Bring salted water to boil. Put mushrooms in boiling water, using wooden
spoon to keep them under water at all times (otherwise they will turn
dark). Keep boiling 3 to 5 minutes, depending on size. (Do not overcook).
Drain and cool quickly. Place in jars and cover with the following mixture:
2 parts salad oil to 1 part cider vinegar; 1 teaspoon salt per quart jar; a few
grains of pepper per jar; pinch of dried parsley flakes per jar; a mashed
clove of garlic per jar; pinch of dried oregano per jar. Shake mixture well
before adding mushrooms. Let stand two days before using! Important:
Shake frequently during the 2 days. *My most requested recipe over many
years. I believe it was originally similar to one used at General Glover in
Swampscott, Massachusetts. Cooked, frozen artichokes may be added as
mushrooms are used. May also be used as salad dressing with or without
mushrooms and artichokes. May be refrigerated.*

Nell Pearson
Silver Spring, Maryland

PICKLED HERRING

Herring fillets
2 parts vinegar
1 part water

1 sliced raw onion
½ cup sugar
1 package pickling spice

Put fillets in heavy brine (Kosher salt) for one week. Wash fillet well to
remove salt. In a crock, layer fish with mixture of vinegar, water, onion,
sugar, and pickling spice. Let fish stand for another week.

Bob Bennett
Cape May, New Jersey

CROUSTADES AUX CHAMPIGNONS
(Mushrooms Croustades)

Crust
24 slices fresh thin sliced bread

Filling

4 tablespoons butter
3 tablespoons finely chopped
  shallots
1 tablespoon finely chopped
  parsley
1½ tablespoons finely chopped
  chives
2 tablespoons Parmesan cheese

2 tablespoons flour
½ pound finely chopped
  mushrooms
1 cup heavy cream
½ teaspoon lemon juice
Pinch: salt, black pepper, cayenne
  pepper

Cut out 3-inch rounds of bread. Butter muffin tins. Place round bread carefully into tins, molding bread to form cup. Bake at 400 degrees for 10 minutes. Remove; cool. In a skillet melt 4 tablespoons butter. Stir in 2 tablespoons flour. Cook shallots 3 minutes; add mushrooms. Stir 15 minutes. Remove from heat. Pour 1 cup cream over mixture. Return to heat; bring to boil. When mixture thickens, turn heat to simmer, for 1 to 2 minutes. Remove from heat add parsley, cheese, lemon juice, spices. Stir well. Place in bowl to cool. When ready to fill croustades sprinkle with Parmesan lightly, dot with speck of butter. Heat croustades at 350 degrees for 10 minutes on cookie sheet. Then place under broiler briefly. Yields 2 dozen. *Borrowed in Bowie, Maryland.*

Sandra McKinely

OLIVE CHEDDAR NUGGET SNACKERS

¼ cup soft margarine
1 cup shredded Cheddar cheese
¾ cup flour

¼ teaspoon salt
½ teaspoon paprika
Small stuffed olives

Mix cheese and flour to form a dough. Add dash of Worcestershire sauce. Shape dough by teaspoon around small stuffed olives. Bake on ungreased cookie sheet for 12 to 15 minutes. Yield 2 to 2½ dozen. *Can be prepared the day before and baked just before serving. Also good when reheated.*

Ada Tuttle

ONION STRIPS

1 loaf sliced bread
1 package onion soup mix

1 cup butter or margarine,
    softened

Cut crust from bread. Mix dry onion soup with butter or margarine. Spread mixture on each slice of bread. Cut each slice into four strips. Toast in oven at 350 degrees for 10 minutes. Serves 20. *These freeze well before baking. Can be made ahead and kept on aluminum foil baking sheet in freezer until ready to bake and serve.*

Jessie Lisk
Springfield, Pennsylvania

PARTY RYE SLICES

Party rye bread
1 red onion, cut in slices

3 tablespoons mayonnaise
1 tablespoon Parmesan cheese

Put 1 slice red onion on piece of party rye. Mix mayonnaise and cheese together. Spread over onion. Put under broiler until brown and bubbly. Serves 8 to 10. *So easy and so good.*

Ann Tourison

PIROSKI

1 can chopped corned beef
2 small onions
1 clove garlic
½ cup grated cheese

2 tablespoons butter
6 to 12 drops hot pepper sauce
Canned biscuit dough
1 egg beaten

Heat oven to 450 degrees. Mix all ingredients except egg. Open and spread out a can of biscuits. Roll thin and cut in 3-inch squares. Place filling in center of each square. Bring up corners and pinch edges together. Brush with egg. Bake 12 minutes. Serves 16. *This is a Russian recipe.*

Blanche Rogers
Jax Beach, Florida

SALMON MOUSSE

1 package gelatin
½ cup boiled water
2 tablespoons lemon juice
1 slice onion
½ cup mayonnaise

1 (1-pound) can salmon (skinned
    and deboned)
¼ teaspoon paprika
1 teaspoon dill
1 cup heavy cream

Dissolve gelatin in water. Pour into blender and add all the remaining ingredients except the cream. Cover and blend while adding the cream. Mixture will be thick and won't splatter. Pour into a greased mold (fish mold sprayed with PAM⁽ᴿ⁾). Chill for 3 to 4 hours. After unmolding onto a large platter arrange parsley and cherry tomatoes around edge. Use an olive slice for eyes. Serve with crackers. Serves 15 to 20 for an hors d'oeuvre.

Patricia Rafftesaeth
Lansdale, Pennsylvania

SALMON MOLD

1½ tablespoons gelatin
½ cup cold water
1 can condensed tomato soup
2 (3-ounce) packages cream
    cheese

1 cup mayonnaise
½ cup chopped onion
2 large cans salmon

Dissolve gelatin in cold water. Bring soup to boil; add cheese and stir until melted; remove from heat. Add gelatin; stir until dissolved. Add mayonnaise, celery, onion and salmon. Pour into fish mold and chill until set. Serves: 10 to 12. *This recipe makes a large quantity. One large and two small molds may be used. Can be served as an hors d'oeuver or salad.*

Jessie Lisk

SEAFOOD CANAPES

4 white fish fillets (flounder, bass)   ½ pound bacon

Cut raw fillets into narrow strips. Cut bacon strips in half. Roll each fish piece in bacon, skewer with toothpick. Broil 5 minutes. Turn, broil, 5 minutes more. Serve with sweet/sour dip if desired, but not necessary. Serves 8 to 10. *This is my own creation the result of having lots of fresh fish around.*

Ms. Loret Smith
Cold Springs, New Jersey

SHRIMP DIP

1 large package cream cheese, softened
3 or more tablespoons chili sauce (bottled)
½ cup mayonnaise
¼ teaspoon Worcestershire sauce

¼ teaspoon or more lemon juice
¼ teaspoon onion juice (or ½ onion, chopped fine)
½ pound shrimp, mashed (you can use 3 or 4 cans shrimp, rinsed and drained)

Mix all, then add more chili sauce or lemon juice as needed. The more shrimp the better. Yields about 2 to 2½ cups. *Grace Kelly gave this recipe to me when we were neighbors in Ocean City.*

Beverly Rauch

SHRIMP DIP

1 can undiluted tomato soup
1 (8-ounce) package cream cheese, softened
1 envelope unflavored gelatin
1 cup finely chopped celery

¼ cup finely chopped onion
½ cup mayonnaise
1 pound cooked shrimp cut up

Dissolve gelatin in ¼ cup water (not hot). Combine tomato soup and cream cheese. Add to gelatin. Heat until smooth on very low temperature, stirring constantly to prevent lumps. Fold in remaining ingredients and chill. Serve on your favorite crackers. Serves 12.

Trudy Jarret
Jax Beach, Florida

SHRIMP BUTTER

½ cup butter, softened
¼ cup mayonnaise

1 small can deveined shrimp
½ teaspoon Jane's Crazy Salt

To butter add mayonnaise, shrimp, salt. Mix. Form into log, freeze. Defrost when needed as quick spread for crackers.

K.C. Bennett

STILTON OR BLUE CHEESE WAFERS

¾ pound cheese
3 tablespoons melted butter

1½ cups sifted flour
2 teaspoons celery seed

Finely mash cheese, add melted butter and celery seed. Add flour and mix to form a dough. Shape dough into 2 logs, wrap in foil and refrigerate 1 hour. Slice dough into ¼-inch thick rounds. Place on baking sheet. put in preheated 400 degree oven and bake approximately 10 minutes or until browned. Yield about 45 biscuits. *Very good with wine or fruit salad.*

K.C. Bennett

STUFFED BREAD

1 large long French bread
2 (8-ounce) packages cream
  cheese
½ pound liverwurst
¼ cup beer

1 tablespoon dry mustard
¼ cup chopped watercress
¼ cup chopped onions
¼ cup chopped radishes

Heat oven to 350 degrees. Cut bread in thirds crosswise. Slice off ends. Scoop out center, leaving about ¼-inch. Crumble dough and toast 15 minutes until brown. Cut liverwurst in small cubes. Stir cream cheese until smooth and soft. Mix beer and mustard and stir into cream cheese and add watercress, onions and radishes. Add liverwurst, mix lightly. When crumbs are cool stir into mixture. Pack into bread, wrap and refrigerate at least four hours. Unwrap and cut into thin slices. Serves 16 to 20. *Hors d'oeuvre goes well at brunch or lunch with Bloody Marys, but good any time. If I can make it, anybody can.*

May McLaughlin

SWISS CHEESE PUFFS

Party Rye or Pumpernickel
½ cup mayonnaise
1 tablespoon chopped parsley

⅓ cup chopped onion
Swiss cheese slices

Mix together mayonnaise, parsley and onion. Spread on bread. Put slices of Swiss cheese on top on cookie sheet. Broil at 350 degrees or 400 degrees until cheese melts and bubbles. Yields about 3½ to 4 dozen.

Barry and Cathy Rein, Columns By the Sea

TANGY SPREAD

1 (10-ounce) jar apricot jam
1 (10-ounce) jar pineapple jam
½ can dry mustard (1.02 ounce)

1 (5-ounce) jar horseradish
(drained)

Mix all together. Serve on crackers. Yield about 3 cups.

Mrs. Robert Brown
Bluebell, Pennsylvania

VEGGIE DIP

2 packages frozen chopped
  spinach, thawed and drained
  well
½ pint sour cream (1 cup)

1 cup mayonnaise
1 package vegetable soup mix
1 can water chestnuts, drained
  and chopped fine

Combine all ingredients, mix well, chill and serve with wheat thins, Yields about 3½ to 4 cups.

Joan Schaeffner

SPARKLING APRICOT PINEAPPLE PUNCH

3 quarts apricot nectar
3 quarts pineapple juice,
  unsweetened
1½ cups frozen lemon or lime
  juice concentrate

2 quarts water
2 quarts gingerale (champagne
  can be substituted)

Combine juices and water. Chill. Just before serving, add ginger ale. Serves 50.

Kate Cronkite
Chicago, Illinois

WHISKEY SOUR PUNCH

2 (6-ounce) cans frozen lemonade
  concentrate
2 (6-ounce) cans frozen orange
  juice concentrate

2 (18-ounce) cans pineapple juice
1 fifth whiskey
2 (28-ounce) bottles gingerale

One hour before party, fill punch bowl three quarters full with concentrates, juice and ice. Before guests arrive, add whiskey and gingerale. Serves 24.

Rona Craig

CHAMPAGNE PUNCH

1 (12-ounce) can frozen orange
  juice concentrate, thawed
1 (12-ounce) can frozen lemonade
  concentrate, thawed

1 quart apple juice
6 cups water
2 bottles champagne, chilled

Combine all ingredients except champagne. Chill 4 to 6 hours. Add chilled champagne to juice mixture in large punch bowl. Serves 25.

Sandra Dickinson
Lansdowne, Pennsylvania

SLUSH PUNCH

1 (12-ounce) large can frozen orange breakfast drink concentrate

1 (12-ounce) large can lemonade frozen concentrate

2 cups double strength tea (4 tea bags)

2 cups granulated sugar

3 or 4 cups whiskey

5 cups water

Mix well and freeze in wide mouth glass or plastic container. When ready to serve scoop into tall glass ½ full, then add 7-up or gingerale. Serves 25. *Delicious summer drink.*

Loretta Baver
Pennsburg, Pennsylvania

MOCHA MILK PUNCH

1 quart coffee ice cream, divided

2 cups strong coffee, chilled and divided

2 cups milk, divided

½ cup bourbon, divided

½ cup rum, (optional) divided

½ cup creme de cacao, divided

Additional coffee ice cream

Sweet chocolate curls

Combine half of all ingredients, except ice cream, in container of electric blender; process until smooth, repeat procedure with remaining ingredients, except extra ice cream, sprinkle with chocolate curls. Serves 20. *From the Southern Heritage "Socials & Soirees" Cookbook. Absolutely delicious. Excellent to serve at a coffee or brunch.*

Vernice Caprio
Villas, New Jersey

MARGUERITAS

1 (6-ounce) can frozen limeade
   concentrate
1 can (use limeade can) Tequilla
   (or little less)

⅓ can Triple Sec
1 egg white

Put above in blender and fill with ice to about 1-inch or 2-inch from top of blender. Add a little water if needed. Blend well until light and foamy and icy. Wet rim of serving glasses and dip in salt if desired. Serves 6 to 8.

Harry Leaming
Orange, California

CHOCOLATE IRISH CREAM

1 cup good quality whiskey
1 (14-ounce) can sweetened
   condensed milk
1 cup heavy cream

4 eggs
½ cup chocolate syrup
2 teaspoons instant coffee
2 teaspoon vanilla extract

Combine all ingredients in blender until smooth. Chill to blend flavors. Stir before serving. Serve over ice if desired. Serves 15. *Store covered in refrigerator for up to one month - great gift in pretty decanter tied with ribbon.*

Liz Mauceri
Southampton, New York

HOLIDAY EGGNOG

4 eggs
1 pint heavy cream
1 quart half and half

½ teaspoon cinnamon
2 tablespoons sugar
Dash of nutmeg and cloves

Beat eggs in blender with sugar, cinnamon, spices. Gradually add cream and half and half. Beat until light and fluffy. Add rum if desired. Serve well chilled. Garnish with cinnamon sticks. Rich and delicious. Serves 6 to 8. *Better than any store bought!*

Grace Yothers
Glenside, Pennsylvania

FLORIDA SUNSHINE PUNCH

1 quart burgundy wine
1 quart orange juice
1 pint grapefruit juice

1 pint water
Sugar to taste

Heat the water and add sugar to make a single syrup. Mix the wine, orange juice and grapefruit juice. Slowly add the syrup until it tastes sweet enough to you. Serve it over ice and garnish with slice of orange, lime or lemon. Add a sprig of mint. Serves 10 to 12. *It's good, but like the Florida sun, do not get too much.*

H. David Reeves
Jax Beach, Florida

RUM SLUSH

2 cups boiling water
1 cup sugar
3 cups light rum
2 cups strong tea
2 cups water

1 (12-ounce) can frozen lemonade
   concentrate
1 (6-ounce) can frozen orange
   juice concentrate

Combine boiling water and sugar in large plastic container and stir until sugar is dissolved. Add remaining ingredients and mix thoroughly. Cover and freeze overnight. Spoon mixture (slush) into glasses. Garnish with mint/lemon slice/whatever - be creative - and serve. Serves a porch full! *It ain't julep-but it's the next best thing on our porch in the summer.*

V.C. Enck

SWEDISH CHRISTMAS GLOGG

3 quarts dry red wine
1 pint sweet vermouth
1 cup sugar
1 cup dark seedless raisins
1 cup golden raisins
6 to 10 whole cardamom, crushed

10 cloves
1 cinnamon stick, broken
Peel of one orange
1 quart vodka or aquavit
2 cups blanched almonds (whole)
Orange slices for garnish

In a large saucepan combine wine, vermouth, sugar, raisins, cardamon, cloves, orange peel, and cinnamon. Bring to boil, reduce heat and simmer 15 minutes. Cool and pour into a large bowl. Let stand at least 12 hours to blend the flavors. Just before serving, return to saucepan and reheat. Add vodka or aquavit and almonds. Pour into heat resistant punch bowl, allowing spices to settle at bottom. Garnish with orange slices. Serves 50.

Elizabeth Von Schlichten

SUPER CIDER FLOAT

1 quart chilled apple cider   Ground nutmeg
1 pint vanilla ice cream

Pour 1 cup of cider in 4 old-fashioned mugs or tall glasses. Top each with a scoop of ice cream. Sprinkle with nutmeg. Serves 4. *Tastes like apple pie a la mode in a glass!*

Betsy Craig

ORANGE EGGNOG

2 (32-ounce) cans of eggnog   1 cup cold water
  (chilled)   Optional: ¾ cups of rum and
2 (6-ounce) cans frozen orange   orange twist
  juice concentrate, thawed

In a large pitcher combine eggnog, water, orange juice, concentrate and rum. Garnish with orange twists. Refrigerate leftovers. Serves 20.

Elizabeth Von Schlichten

Soups, Salads
and
Sandwiches

Roof Tops

The nation's oldest seashore resort welcomes you with echoes
from the past. Cupolas, gables, mansards, steeples, turrets,
and widow's walks are the crowning glories of a concentration
of magnificent Victorian architecture.

ASPARAGUS VICHYSSOISE

2 pounds fresh asparagus
3 or 4 scallions, chopped
2 cups diced and peeled potato
3 cups water
3 chicken flavored bouillon cubes

¾ cup skim milk
¼ teaspoon salt
⅛ teaspoon white pepper
4 dashes hot sauce
Lemon rind curls

Snap tough ends from asparagus and remove scales if desired. Cut asparagus in l-inch strips, reserving tips. Cook asparagus tips in boiling water until tender; then drain and chill. Combine asparagus pieces, scallions, potato, water and bouillon cubes in large saucepan and bring to boil. Cover and simmer until tender or approximately 25 minutes. Place mixture in blender or processor until smooth. Pour into large bowl and stir in milk, salt, pepper and hot sauce. Chill. Ladle into chilled soup bowls. Garnish with tips and lemon rind curls and serve immediately. Serves 5. *Great for a low calorie (120) soup.*

Donna Gaver Shank
Dover, Delaware

CELERY SOUP

l bunch of celery
l large onion
Chicken bouillon cubes

3 tablespoons flour
l cup milk

Wash and cut up a bunch of celery and one big onion. Cover with water in a large pot and boil until quite well done (an hour or more). Put the celery and onion mixture into blender (not the liquid) and blend. Add one chicken bouillon cube for each cup of remaining liquid in the pot. Pour the pureed celery back into the liquid. Mix about 3 tablespoons of flour with about a cup of milk until smooth. Stir gradually into the simmering soup. Let it simmer before serving. Serves 4. *This is very easy and can be made ahead.*

Lydia M. Magee

CRAB BISQUE

1 (10¼-ounce) can cream
  mushroom soup
1½ soup cans milk

1 cup heavy cream
1 (8-ounce) container crabmeat
¼ cup sherry

Stir soup, milk and cream together. Heat just to boiling. Add crabmeat. Heat thoroughly. Stir in sherry. Just before serving float butter on top. Serves 4 to 6. *The flavor is enhanced if allowed to set.*

Tom Williams

CREAM OF MUSHROOM SOUP

½ cup butter
½ cup onions, chopped
½ cup celery, chopped
¼ cup carrots, chopped
1¾ pounds mushrooms, chopped
¾ cup flour

3 cups chicken stock
2 cups milk
¼ teaspoon nutmeg
⅛ teaspoon paprika
2 tablespoons parsley, chopped
Sherry to taste

Saute onions, celery and carrots in butter. Add mushrooms and remaining ingredients. Simmer for a few minutes before serving. Serves 6.

FISH CHOWDER

3 to 4 large fish fillets (bluefish,
  weakfish, or cod)
2 cans Cheddar cheese soup
2 cans cream of celery soup
1 can water

½ cup butter or margarine
1 large chopped onion
1 stalk celery, chopped
Salt and pepper to taste
1 cup sherry (optional)

Boil fillets in water 10 minutes. Cool and flake. Saute onion, celery in butter. Add to soups and water in large pot. Add fish, stir and heat. Serves 8.

Jack and Lou Conine
Stone Harbor, New Jersey

FRENCH ONION SOUP

3 large Spanish onions, thinly
   sliced
3 cans consomme
½ can water
1 teaspoon salt
1 teaspoon dark brown gravy
   sauce

1 tablespoon Worcestershire sauce
4 tablespoons butter (½ stick)
Salt and pepper to taste
Grated Parmesan cheese
French bread, toasted
Swiss cheese

Melt butter in heavy pot with lid. Place onions in butter and cook slowly with lid on. Put in salt when onions start to cook. When onions are thoroughly cooked (about 1 hour), add seasoning, water and consomme. Bring to a boil and simmer 30 minutes. Brown thinly sliced French bread on one side, put Swiss cheese on untoasted side and brown. Put soup in bowls, dividing onions equally. Float toasted bread on top. Serve with Parmesan cheese. Serves 6.

HANNAH'S HOMEMADE SOUP

2 to 3 pounds short ribs of beef
½ cup barley
1 tablespoon pot herbs
1 to 2 onions, diced
1 (28-ounce) can peeled tomatoes

2 pounds carrots
6 to 8 potatoes
1 (17-ounce) can whole corn
1 (16-ounce) can cut green beans
1 (17-ounce) can small sweet peas

In an 8-quart pot, add 2 quarts of water, short ribs, barley, pot herbs, onions and tomatoes. Simmer 2½ hours. Add peeled and diced carrots and potatoes. Cook ½ hour. Remove meat and any bones that may have come loose. Add, including their liquids, the corn, beans and peas. Cut up meat and return to pot. Simmer 5 to 10 minutes to heat vegetables through. Serves 30 (8-ounce). *My mother, Hannah Greener began making this soup 60 years ago. It's a meal in itself and great with rye or Italian bread.*

Joan Porter
Churchville, Pennsylvania

MANHATTAN CLAM CHOWDER

4 bacon strips
4 medium onions, diced
4 carrots, diced
1 stalk celery, diced
Few parsley sprigs, chopped
1 (1-pound and 14-ounce) can
  tomatoes

1 pint clams, chopped
2 teaspoons salt
4 peppercorns
1 bay leaf
½ teaspoon thyme
3 medium finely diced potatoes

Cut bacon in small pieces and fry in a large kettle until almost crisp. Toss in onions and cook until limp. Add carrots, celery and parsley. Cook over low heat for 5 minutes. Stir occasionally. Add tomatoes. Add clam liquid and enough water to make 1½ quarts. Season with herbs and spices. Cook to a boil, then reduce heat, cover and cook gently for 45 minutes. Add potatoes, cover and cook 20 minutes longer. Add clams and cook slowly, uncovered for 15 minutes. Makes 3 quarts of chowder. *Tastes even better when reheated the second day.*

Deborah Guilloz
Southampton, New York

NEW ENGLAND CORN CHOWDER

5 slices of bacon
1 medium onion, thinly sliced
2 cups of cooked or canned whole
  kernel corn
1 cup of diced or thinly sliced
  cooked potatoes

1 (10½-ounce) can condensed
  cream of mushroom soup
2½ cups of milk
1 teaspoon of salt or to taste
Dash of pepper

Cook bacon until crisp in large sauce pan. Remove bacon and pour off all but 3 tablespoons of drippings. Add onion separated into rings. Cook until lightly browned. Add remaining ingredients and a dash of pepper. Heat to boiling (a little longer if raw potatoes are used); simmer a minute or two. Top servings with crumbled bacon and butter. Serves 6. *This is an easy recipe and it can be frozen.*

Edith S. Lemmon

BEEF STOCK LENTIL SOUP

1½ cups lentils
6 cups beef stock
2 large tomatoes, chopped
1 clove of garlic, pressed
1 teaspoon caraway seed
1 onion, thinly sliced

2 tablespoons margarine
1 tablespoon lemon juice
Salt to taste
Allspice to taste
Lemon slices

Rinse the lentils in cold water until the water is clear. Place in a sauce pan and add the beef stock, tomatoes, chopped onion, garlic and caraway seed. Bring to a boil, then reduce heat and simmer for about 1 hour. Fry the sliced onion in the margarine until light brown, then drain on an absorbent paper. Mash the soup through a strainer, then pour back into the saucepan and heat through. Season with lemon juice, salt, and allspice. Serve with lemon slices and fried onion. Serves 6 to 8.

CREAM OF PARSNIP SOUP

3 parsnips, peeled, diced or sliced
1 onion, chopped
2 stalks celery, diced or sliced
2½ cups chicken stock

⅛ teaspoon curry powder
1 cup heavy cream
Chives

Boil all ingredients except cream. Puree, season and add cream. Serves 4.

Anita Laird

CREAM OF PEANUT SOUP
King's Arms Tavern

1 medium onion, chopped
2 ribs of celery, chopped
¼ cup butter
3 tablespoons all-purpose flour

2 quarts chicken stock or broth
2 cups smooth peanut butter
1¾ cups light cream
Peanuts, chopped

Saute onion and celery in butter until soft, but not brown. Stir in flour until well blended. Add chicken stock, stirring constantly and bring to a boil. Remove from heat. Blend in blender and rub through a sieve. Add peanut butter and cream, stirring to blend thoroughly. Return to low heat, but do not boil. Serve garnished with peanuts. Serves 8.

"ERWTEN SOEP"
Dutch Pea Soup

1 pound green peas
20 cups water
2 pig hocks
4 green onions

3 or 4 leeks
1 bunch of celery
½ pound smoked sausage
2 teaspoon salt

Soak peas overnight and boil them in the same water with pig hocks, salt, chopped celery and thinly sliced leeks. Stirring regularly boil until the soup thickens and the meat drops from the bones (about 3 hours). Boil the sausage in the soup for the last ½ hour. Serves 20 8-ounce. *A winter favorite. Erwten soep (pea soup) is to the Dutch what fried chicken is to Americans. It is not uncommon to find this rich green pea soup dotted with smoked sausage being offered from wooded roadhouses along frozen Dutch canals.*

Carin Fedderman and Milly La Canfora, Capt. Mey's Inn

PUMPKIN SOUP

7 tablespoons butter
6 scallions, chopped
1 onion, sliced
2½ pounds pumpkin, diced or 3
   cups pumpkin puree
6 cups chicken broth

½ teaspoon salt
1 cup light cream
3 tablespoons flour
Lightly salted whipped cream
Croutons

Melt 4 tablespoons butter in large saucepan. Saute scallions and onion until soft and golden. Add pumpkin, broth and salt. Bring to boil, stirring. Rub soup through fine sieve or strain puree if whole pumpkin is used. Return to pan. Knead flour with 2 tablespoons butter. Add, gradually to soup, beating with whisk. Bring soup to boil, whipping until thick. Correct seasoning. Add light cream and remaining butter. Serve garnished with croutons and whipped cream. Serves 8. *I always used canned pumpkin. It's always uniform and saves time.*

Rebekah Martin

SEAFOOD CHOWDER

1 cup heavy cream
1½ stalks celery
1½ pounds carrots
2 medium onions
1 (46-ounce) tomato juice
1 cup white wine

1 cup half-and-half
2½ pounds monkfish
1 tablespoon salt
1 tablespoon pepper
¼ cup butter

Cuisinart all vegetables until fine and saute in butter over low heat. Add 46 ounce tomato juice and 1 cup of wine. Bring to a boil. When soup boils add finely diced monkfish, salt and pepper. Lower heat and simmer covered for 1½ hours. At this point it may be cooled for storage or freezing, or used immediately by adding heavy cream and half-and-half.

The Shire

SEAFOOD CHOWDER

3 cups cooked seafood (shrimp,
    scallops, clams, crab)
6 tablespoons butter
6 tablespoons flour
1½ cups milk
½ cup dry sherry

8 drops Worcestershire
½ teaspoon pepper
¼ cup chopped leeks (or green
    onions)
1 cup fresh mushrooms

In a heavy gauge saucepan, melt butter. Mix flour and slowly add milk. Stir frequently to keep lump free. Cook over medium heat until liquid boils and becomes thickened. Add sherry, Worcestershire and pepper. Simmer for 2 minutes. In another pan, saute leeks and mushrooms. Add to liquid. Add cooked seafood and heat until warmed. Serve 4 to 6.

Claire Sandbach
Wilmington, Delaware

NASSAU SEAFOOD CHOWDER

1½ pounds scallops
1 green pepper
1 carrot
½ teaspoon thyme
2 large onions
1 (1-pound 15-ounce) can whole
  tomatoes

½ can tomato paste
1 cup soda cracker crumbs
48 ounces clam juice
Salt and pepper to taste
4 tablespoons butter, halved
2 tablespoons all-purpose flour
½ cup cream sherry

Coarsely grind scallops, pepper, carrots and onions. Saute in 2 tablespoons butter for 10 minutes. Add thyme. Cut tomatoes, saving the juice. Add tomatoes, juice and paste to fish mixture. Add saltine crumbs and clam juice. Stir well. Cook slowly for 1 hour. Make a roux with 2 tablespoons butter and flour. Add a small amount of soup then return to soup to thicken. Add sherry just before serving. Serves 6 to 8.

Betty Deal
Medford, New Jersey

VEGETABLE SOUP

2 pounds beef shin meat
Large beef bone
Small cabbage, finely cut
2 (10-ounce) packages frozen peas
2 (10-ounce) packages frozen corn
2 (10-ounce) packages frozen lima
  beans

3 stalks celery, chopped
4 carrots, chopped
2 cans tomato soup
2 10-ounce cans whole tomatoes
  (undrained)
Large pinch of pot herbs
Parsley, chopped

Brown meat with bone. Add water, vegetables, pot herbs and parsley. Cook about 3 hours. Remove bone and meat. Chop meat in small pieces and return to pot. Serves 10. *Very easy and can be made days ahead.*

Ann Tourison

ARTICHOKE RICE SALAD

1 package chicken flavored rice
   mix (or about 6 cups of rice
   cooked in bouillon cubes)
4 green onions, sliced thinly
½ green pepper, seeded and
   chopped

12 sliced pimiento-stuffed olives
2 (6-ounce) jars marinated
   artichoke hearts
¾ teaspoon curry powder
⅓ cup mayonnaise

Cook rice as directed on package (omitting butter). Cool in large bowl. Add green onions, green pepper, olives. Drain artichoke hearts, reserving marinade, and chop coarsely. Combine artichoke marinade with curry powder and mayonnaise. Add artichoke hearts to rice salad and toss with dressing. Chill. Serves 10 to 12.

Peggy Madden, Dormer House International

CHRISTMAS SALAD
(My Grandmother's and My Favorite)

1 cup diced canned red beets
1¼ cups diced cooked potatoes
1 cup diced cooked ham
1 pickle finely diced
1½ apples, pared and diced
2 tablespoons vinegar
1 teaspoon sugar

⅛ teaspoon white pepper
1 hard boiled egg separated
Parsley
Cooked small beets
¼ cup whipping cream
½ cup sour cream

Mix diced beets, potatoes, ham, pickle and apples. Add vinegar, sugar and white pepper. Turn out on serving platter. Chop egg whites into strips and arrange in spiral on top of salad. Mash egg yolks and spoon into center. Garnish with parsley and small beets. Serve with whipped or sour cream. Serves 8 to 12. *In Sweden we sometimes also add chopped pickled herring to this dish and serve ice cold aquavit with it (only one small glass please).*

Elizabeth von Schlichten

COBB SALAD

10 cups shredded lettuce
3½ to 4 cups chopped cooked
  chicken
6 hard-cooked eggs, chopped

3 large tomatoes, chopped
2 ripe avocados, chopped
¾ cup crumbled, crisp bacon
2½ cups bleu cheese, crumbled

Line very large bowl with lettuce. Arrange other ingredients in rows on top.

Vinaigrette
3 tablespoons red wine vinegar
1 cup vegetable oil
¼ cup lemon juice
1 heaping tablespoon sugar
1 teaspoon dry mustard

½ teaspoon salt
1 teaspoon Worcestershire sauce
1 teaspoon garlic, minced
½ teaspoon lemon pepper

Shake all ingredients in a covered container. Refrigerate at least 1 hour. Serve with salad. Serves 6 to 8.

Jeannie Lukk
Elkton, Maryland

HEARTS OF PALM SALAD

1 (1-pound) can hearts of palm,
  chilled and drained
Crisp Romaine lettuce leaves
6 pimiento stuffed olives, sliced
2 teaspoons green peppercorns in
  vinegar (optional)

2 tablespoons salted nuts,
  chopped
Paprika
Italian dressing

Cut hearts of palm lengthwise. Place on crisp lettuce leaves. Garnish with olive slices and green peppercorns. Sprinkle salted nuts and paprika on top. Serves 2.

Elizabeth von Schlichten

CUCUMBER MOUSSE

8 cucumbers
1 medium onion, grated
4 tablespoons unflavored gelatin
2 cups cucumber liquid
Juice of 2 lemons

2 cups whipped cream, whipped
1 cup mayonnaise
1 cup sour cream
4 tablespoons fresh chopped dill

Oil your favorite 8 cup mold. Peel cucumbers, cut lengthwise, remove seeds, and coarsely grate them into a bowl lined with a turkish towel. Add 1 tablespoon salt to grated cucumbers and mix together. Allow to set for ½ hour. Gently gather ends of towel and squeeze liquid from cucumbers into bowl. Save liquid. 2 cups are needed and add water if necessary. Boil 1 cup of cucumber liquid. Take remaining 1 cup of cucumber liquid to softened gelatin mixture and stir well until all gelatin is dissolved. Set aside. In a large bowl add squeezed out cucumbers, lemon juice, grated onion, mayonnaise, sour cream, dill, salt, pepper, gelatin, and cucumber liquid. Fold in whipped cream. Pour into mold. Refrigerate at least 6 hours, preferably overnight. Remove from mold and decorate with scored cucumber slices and lemon. Serves 12 to 16. *A refreshing summer salad which can also be very decorative when prepared in your favorite shaped mold and decorated accordingly.*

Bonita Wolchko-Rivera
Bryn Athyn, Pennsylvania

GREEN BEAN AND POTATO SALAD

1 tablespoon bacon fat
½ to ⅓ cup of mayonnaise
2 tablespoons fresh lemon juice
1¼ teaspoon salt
⅛ teaspoon fresh ground pepper
⅛ teaspoon garlic powder
1 pound cooked green beans or
    frozen green beans

4 medium potatoes cooked and
    diced
1½ cups diced celery
½ cup chopped onion
4 slices crisp bacon

Combine first six ingredients and heat. Mix green beans, potatoes, celery and onion, toss lightly with hot dressing. Garnish with crisp bacon crumbled over top. Serves 6 to 8.

Doris Jardin

BROCCOLI SALAD

2 packages fresh broccoli (florets
   only)
½ cup oil
1 sliced green pepper
4 cups sliced mushrooms

1 can bean sprouts
1 can sliced water chestnuts
½ cup vinegar
¼ cup soy sauce
2½ teaspoon salt

Pan fry broccoli with ½ cup oil. Add pepper and mushrooms. Cook 2 to 3 minutes. In large bowl add all other ingredients. Toss with broccoli mix and chill. Serves 8.

Claire Menge

BROCCOLI SALAD

1 head broccoli
1 medium red onion
8 ounces shredded Cheddar,
   Swiss or mozzarella cheese

½ pound crisp bacon, crumbled
1 cup mayonnaise
½ cup sugar
2 or 3 tablespoons cider vinegar

Clean and break broccoli into bite size pieces, after peeling stems. Combine with cheese and bacon. Make dressing with mayonnaise, sugar and vinegar. Toss together. Chill before serving. Lasts several days in refrigerator. Serves 6 to 8. *Great salad with picnics. Has Pennsylvania Dutch sweet and sour flavor. Good with seafood.*

Barry and Cathy Rein, Column by the Sea

BROCCOLI SALAD

1 head of broccoli
⅓ cup mayonnaise
⅓ cup Parmesan cheese

Salt and pepper to taste
Large red onion

Cut broccoli in very small pieces, stem and all. Cut onion in small pieces. Mix with mayonnaise and cheese. Season with salt and pepper. Serves 6.

Ann M. Tourison

CAULIFLOWER SALAD

1 head of lettuce, broken into bite size pieces
1 head cauliflower, broken into little florets
1 sweet small onion

1 pound bacon, diced and fried crisp
1 cup Parmesan cheese, grated
1 cup mayonnaise

Layer in large bowl in above order. Just before serving, toss lightly once or twice. Holds well for camping or picnic. Lettuce stays crisp while unmixed.

Virgina Morrow

OVERNIGHT LAYERED CHICKEN SALAD

6 cups shredded iceberg lettuce
1 (8-ounce) can sliced, drained water chestnuts
¼ pound fresh bean sprouts (or canned, drained)

½ cup green onions, sliced
4 cups cooked diced chicken
2 (9 to 10-ounce) packages frozen pea pods, thawed
1 small cucumber, thinly sliced

Salad Dressing
2 cups mayonnaise
2 teaspoons curry powder

1 tablespoon sugar
½ teaspoon ground ginger

Arrange lettuce in bottom of 13x9-inch dish. Top with layers of sprouts, water chestnuts, onions, chicken, cucumbers and pea pods on top. In small bowl stir together salad dressing ingredients. Spread evenly over pea pods. Cover tightly with plastic wrap and refrigerate overnight. Before serving, garnish with halved cherry tomatoes and/or avocado slices. Serves 8 to 10.

Mary Edwards
Bedford, New Hampshire

SOY CHICKEN SALAD

4 tablespoons coarse chopped
  ginger root
2 chicken breasts, halved
4 tablespoons soy sauce
2 tablespoons sherry
4 teaspoons sesame oil

½ teaspoons red pepper flakes
2 teaspoons sugar
5 tablespoons chopped scallions
5 tablespoons chopped parsley
1 cup chopped water chestnuts

In saucepan put 2 cups water and ginger root with tight lid. Bring to a boil, then simmer 15 minutes. Place chicken, skin side down, in liquid and poach until done (approximately 15 to 20 minutes). Remove and cool. Reserve enough ginger to make 2 teaspoons finely chopped. Combine soy, sherry, sesame oil, pepper flakes, sugar and reserved ginger. Shred chicken meat very fine (discard skin). Add to soy mix. Toss in scallions, parsley and water chestnuts. Mix well. Chill at least 2 to 3 hours (best overnight). Serve on bed of Bibb lettuce. Serves 4 to 6.

Arlene Fornabaio, Catering

CHICKEN SALAD HABANA

1½ cups boned, cooked chicken in
  thin strips
1 cup ripe olives, sliced
1 avocado cut into crescents

⅓ green pepper strips
½ cup red onion finely chopped
4 cups lettuce, shredded

Dressing
⅓ cup salad oil
¼ cup red wine vinegar
¼ cup lemon juice
1 tablespoon sugar

1 teaspoon salt
½ teaspoon pepper
⅛ to ¼ teaspoon fresh minced
  garlic

Combine ingredients except avocado and lettuce. Chill. Combine dressing ingredients and shake well. Refrigerate. Just before serving, add avocados, shake dressing, pour over salad. Toss lightly; serve on bed of shredded lettuce. Serves 4 to 6.

Mary Edwards
Bedford, New Hampshire

MOLDED CHICKEN SALAD

1 small package lemon flavored
   gelatin
1 can heated and undiluted cream
   of chicken soup
⅓ cup lemon juice

1 cup diced chicken
½ cup diced celery
2 tablespoosn grated onion
2 teaspoons chopped olives
½ cup mayonnaise

Dissolve lemon flavored gelatin in heated soup. Mix all ingredients together, turn into pyrex baking dish and chill. Cut into six squares. *I like to make this a day ahead. It will keep for several days.*

Rebekah Martin

LULU SALAD

1 package lemon flavored gelatin
1¾ cup hot water
1 pound cottage cheese
½ cup tart mayonnaise
½ green pepper, chopped
1 cup celery, chopped

½ large onion, chopped
½ teaspoon salt
Pepper to taste
1 envelope unflavored gelatin,
   mixed in ¼ cup water

Mix all together and let set several hours. Cut into squares. May be put into molds for buffet serving. Serves 6 to 8.

Gurd Tolley

MOTHER'S POTATO SALAD

8 medium sized potatoes
1 cup chopped celery
4 hard boiled eggs

Pinch of salt and pepper
½ cup mayonnaise

Dressing
1 cup vinegar
1 cup sugar

1 egg
1 tablespoon cornstarch

Peel and cube potatoes, chop celery. Cook potatoes until almost soft. Add celery. For dressing, mix together vinegar, sugar, 1 egg and cornstarch. Boil until thickens. Pour over potatoes and celery, add hard boiled eggs, salt, pepper, ½ cup mayonnaise. Let salad cool and then refrigerate for 6 hours. Serves 8 to 10.

Audrey A. Goss
Newmanstown, Pennsylvania

ORANGE CREAM FRUIT SALAD

1 (20-ounce) can pineapple chunks,
   drained
1 (16-ounce) can peach slices,
   drained
1 (11-ounce) can Mandarin orange
   sections, drained
3 medium bananas, sliced
2 medium apples, cored and
chopped

1 (3½-ounce) small package instant
   vanilla pudding
1½ cups milk
½ (6-ounce) can frozen orange
   juice concentrate, thawed
¾ cup dairy sour cream
Lettuce

In large bowl combine all fruit and set aside. In small bowl combine dry pudding mix, milk and orange juice concentrate. Beat 1 to 2 minutes or until well blended. Beat in sour cream. Fold into the fruit mixture. Cover and refrigerate several hours. Serve on lettuce. Serves 10 to 12.

Sandy Miller, Windward House

GINGER PEAR SALAD

1 small package lemon flavored
   gelatin
1 cup gingerale
1 (3-ounce) package cream cheese

½ teaspoon ground ginger
½ cup evaporated milk
¾ cup grapes
¾ cup pears, drained

Dissolve lemon gelatin in ½ cup hot water. Stir in gingerale. Mix cream cheese with ginger and milk. Combine milk-cream cheese mixture into gelatin mixture. When slightly thick, beat one minute and fold in grapes and pears. Chill. Serves 4 to 6.

Jan Wood, Woodleigh House

GRANDMA EGELHOFF'S
PINEAPPLE CREAM SALAD

1 7-ounce bottle lemon-lime
   carbonated soda
2½ cups mini marshmallows
1 (6-ounce) box lime flavored
   gelatin
6 ounces cream cheese, softened

Juice from 1 small lemon
Few drops green food coloring
1 (15¼-ounces) can crushed
   pineapple with juice
¾ cup chopped nuts
1 cup whipping cream, whipped

Combine soda and marshmallows in top of double boiler and heat over boiling water until marshmallows are melted. Add gelatin, stir to dissolve. Add soft cream cheese and beat with electric beater until mixture is smooth. Add lemon juice, food coloring and pineapple. Chill until slightly thickened. Fold in nuts and whipped cream. Chill until firm. Serves 6 to 8.

Joan Alvarez

SAUERKRAUT SALAD

2 (29-ounce) cans sauerkraut (do not drain)
1 large chopped onion
1 cup chopped carrots
1 cup chopped celery
1 chopped green pepper
1 cup sugar

Mix all ingredients except sugar. Sprinkle sugar over top of mixture. Cover container and refrigerate 24 hours. Mix well and serve. Serves 6.

CAPE MAY COLE SLAW
For the Microwave

Medium head of shredded cabbage
¾ cup of sugar
2 tablespoon flour
½ teaspoon dry mustard
1 egg
½ cup water
½ cup vinegar
½ cup mayonnaise

Mix sugar, flour and dry mustard in 4 cup pyrex bowl. Stir in 1 egg. Mix well. Stir in water and vinegar. Cover. Microwave on high 2 minutes. Stir. Microwave 2 minutes more. Allow to cool to room temperature. Stir in ½ cup mayonnaise. Chill. Mix with cabbage before serving. Serves 10 to 12. *An old Cape May recipe which I adapted to microwave.*

Sue Leaming

CHOLESTEROL-FREE COLE SLAW

1 medium size head of shredded cabbage
2 medium finely chopped carrots
½ cup of Bright Day Dressing (sold at most markets)

Mix all ingredients together and chill before serving. You can add ¼ cup of sugar to above recipe. Serves 10 to 12.

Mary Prouty
Barrington, New Jersey

SWEET AND SIMPLE COLESLAW

5 cups shredded cabbage
½ cup chopped green pepper
½ cup chopped red pepper
1 cup chopped onions
3 ounces sugar

½ teaspoon celery seed
½ teaspoon dry mustard
1 teaspoon salt
½ cup white vinegar
3 ounces vegetable oil

In large bowl layer cabbage, green and red pepper and onion. Sprinkle sugar over all, reserving one teaspoon. In saucepan combine one teaspoon sugar and remaining ingredients. Mix well and heat to boiling, stirring constantly. Pour over slaw and refrigerate at least 4 hours. Just before serving, toss slaw thoroughly. Tastes like pepper hash. Will last several weeks in refrigerator. Serves 10 to 12.

Marge Bozarth, Sea Holly Inn

CREAMY SUMMER SLAW

⅓ cup mayonnaise
¼ cup vegetable oil
2 tablespoon cider vinegar
1 tablespoon sugar
1 teaspoon Dijon mustard
½ teaspoon celery seed
½ teaspoon fresh ground black
  pepper

½ teaspoon cayenne pepper
1 tablespoon freshly squeezed
  lemon
½ small green cabbage, cored,
  finely shredded (about 4 cups)
2 small zucchini, thinly sliced
2 small yellow squash

In large bowl, combine the mayonnaise, oil, vinegar, lemon, sugar, mustard, celery seed, and peppers. Using a fork, beat until well-blended. Add cabbage, zucchini, and squash. Toss with dressing to coat thoroughly. Refrigerate at least 1 hour before serving. Makes plenty for any gathering. Serves 6 to 8.

Heather H. Warner

THREE BEAN SALAD

1 can green beans, drained
1 can yellow beans, drained
1 can kindney beans, drained
1 cup apple jelly

½ cup cider vinegar
4 teaspoons cornstarch
1 teaspoon salt

Combine beans in a large bowl. Set aside. Combine jelly, vinegar, cornstarch and salt in a small sauce pan. Stir over medium-low heat until slightly thickened. Pour over beans and mix. Refrigerate overnight. Chopped onions or green peppers are also good with the beans and each adds a slightly different taste. Serves 6 to 8.

Dorothy Garrabrant
North Wildwood, New Jersey

OVERNIGHT TOSSED SALAD

1 medium head lettuce
10 ounces fresh spinach
½ cup sliced green onion
1 pint cherry tomatoes, halved

10 ounces frozen peas, thawed
1 pound bacon, cooked, drained,
 diced

Dressing
1½ cup mayonnaise
1 cup sour cream
2 teaspoons lemon juice
½ teaspoon oregano

¼ teaspoon basil
¼ teaspoon salt
½ teaspoon pepper

Combine dressing ingredients and mix well. Spread over salad. Be sure to frost entire surface. Do not mix into salad or it will become soggy. Cover with plastic wrap and refigerate over night. Just before serving, toss gently. Serves 8 to 10.

Virginia Morrow

WHIPPED FRUIT SALAD

Base

1 large (29-ounce) can apricots (peeled)

1 large can crushed pineapple

2 small packages orange flavored gelatin

2 cups hot water

1 cup apricot and pineapple juice (reserved)

¾ cup miniature marshmallows

Topping

½ cup sugar

3 tablespoons flour

1 slightly beaten egg

1 cup fruit juice

2 tablespoons butter

1 cup whipped cream (½ pint)

¾ cup shredded Cheddar cheese

Drain fruit, cut apricots into small pieces. Chill. Dissolve gelatin in hot water and add juice. Chill until only slightly set. Put in fruit and marshmallows. Put in 9x13-inch pan. Chill until firm. Combine sugar and flour in pot. Blend in egg and gradually stir in juice. Cook over low heat-stirring constantly until thick. Remove and stir in butter, cool. Fold in whipped cream. Spread over firm gelatin and then garnish with Cheddar cheese. *I usually prepare this over the course of a couple of days to ensure firmness.* Serves 8 to 10.

M. Edna Andrus
Haddon Township, New Jersey

TACO SALAD

1 large head lettuce

1 large tomato, wedged

1 large green pepper, sliced

1 large onion, sliced

1 (16-ounce) bottle Catalina style dressing

½ pound ground beef

1 large bag tortilla chips

1 large can pinto beans (undrained)

Marinate tomato, green pepper, onion, beans in Catalina dressing overnight. Chop lettuce, crush Doritos. Fry beef (drain off fat). Add together with marinated ingredients. Serves 6.

Tib Lamson

HOT HAM AND CHEESE SANDWICH

18 small soft Kaiser rolls
1 cup melted butter
¼ to ½ cup yellow mustard
2 tablespoons grated onion

1 tablespoon poppy seeds
2 pounds boiled ham, sliced
1 pound American cheese, sliced

Brush inside of rolls with mustard. Mix butter, onion, poppy seeds over low heat. Insert ham and cheese and brush outside of roll with mix. Wrap in foil and freeze. Bake at 350 degrees for 15 minutes. Microwave: 1¼ minutes). Yields 18 sandwiches. *Great for make aheads for parties or quick snacks. Once you try it you'll make them over and over again.*

Maryann Hoagland
Blue Bell, Pennsylvania

CHEESE DREAMS
From Original Mac Cookbook

American cheese for 4 sandwiches
8 slices bread
4 eggs

½ cup milk
Salt and pepper to taste
Margarine or butter

Make 4 cheese sandwiches. Beat eggs and milk together. Season with salt and pepper. Dip entire sandwich into mixture and saute in margarine or butter. You can add ham or bacon and cook in bacon fat. Serves 4. *Puffs up and is delicious!*

INSIDE-OUT SANDWICHES

1 package Lebanon bologna
1 small container soft cream
   cheese

1 package bread sticks

Take meat out of package and dab with paper towel to absorb excess juices. Spread each slice with cream cheese. Place bread stick on top of cream cheese and roll up. This recipe is easy to make and can be used as a light lunch finger food. Serves 4. *You can vary this recipe by using different types of meats or by replacing meat with long green onions.*

Lori Schue

HAM BAR-B-Q'S

1 bottle chili sauce
1 teaspoon Worcestershire sauce
½ cup celery, diced
1 medium onion, diced
1 small clove garlic, crushed
½ cup vinegar

1 small can tomato paste
¾ cup sugar
2 cups water
5 drops hot sauce
1 pound chopped ham

Put all above ingredients in a 2-quart saucepan except the ham. Simmer for one hour, stirring frequently. Add the ham and warm thoroughly before serving. Serve on sandwich rolls. Serves 6 to 8. *This recipe is a family favorite. It has been passed down from my great-grandmother through four generations.*

Patricia Brandstetter
Pittsburgh, Pennsylvania

KENTUCKY HOT BROWNS

Cheese Sauce

2 tablespoons butter
¼ cup all-purpose flour
2 cups milk
¼ cup grated sharp Cheddar

cheese
¼ cup grated Parmesan cheese
Salt to taste
¼ teaspoon Worcestershire sauce

Melt butter in a saucepan, blend in flour. Add milk, cheeses and seasonings, stirring constantly until smooth and thickened. Set aside.

Sandwiches

8 slices toast, trimmed
1 pound sliced turkey breast
8 slices tomato

8 slices partially cooked bacon
4 ounces grated Parmesan cheese

Cut toast in triangles and put in baking dishes. Arrange turkey slices on toast. Top with hot cheese sauce, tomato and bacon in that order. Sprinkle with Parmesan cheese and bake at 400 degrees for approximately 10 minutes or until bubbly. Serves 8.

Rona Craig

Cheese, Eggs, and Pasta

The Stockton Cottages, 1871
Guerney Street

Enjoy the outstanding collection of beautifully detailed houses, complete with lacey trim and Italianate windows. These are classic examples of the Cape May Cottage.

GOOD MIXERS

CHEESE	WINE	FRUIT
Blue, Gorogonzola	Claret, burgundy, port, brandy, chianti, champagne	Pears, apples, oranges peaches
Brie	Dry port, cognac, calvados, burgundy	Pears, apples, peaches nectarines, strawberries
Brick	Roses, white wine, cream sherry	Apples, cantaloupe, apricots, cherries grapes
Camembert	All ports, red wine, pink champagne, cognac	Apples, plums, pineapple grapes
Cheddar	Ports, sherry, madeira, claret, burgundy	Apples, cherries, melon, pears, grapes
Colby	Ports, sherry, madeira, claret, burgundy	Apples, cherries, melon, pears
Cream	Sparkling wines, roses, sweet wine	Oranges, tangerines, preserved kumquats, strawberries
Edam	Tokay, cold duck, claret, muscatel	Apples, grapes, oranges, pineapple
Gouda	Tokay, cold duck, roses	Apples, grapes, oranges, pineapple honeydew
Liederkranz	Dry red wines	Apples, Tokay grapes pears
Limburger	Dry red wines	Apples, Tokay grapes, pears

Monterey Jack	Roses, white wines, cream sherry	Apples, cantaloupe, honeydew, apricots, pears
Muenster	Roses, white wines, cream sherry	Apples, cantaloupe, apricots, cherries, grapes, pears
Neufchatel	Sparkling wines, roses, white wines	Oranges, tangerines
Port du Salut	Red, white or roses, light, dry and fruity	Apples, pears
Provolone	Dry red, dry white	Green grapes, apples, pears
Stilton	Fruit wines, port burgundy, cognac, Sherry	Oranges, tangerines
Swiss	Sauterne, brut (dry) champagne, dry or sweet white wine sparkling burgundy	Oranges, tangerines, pineapple

BACON AND CHEESE PUFF

1 pound bacon
1 (8-ounce) can refrigerator
　crescent rolls
2 medium tomatoes, sliced
6 to 8 slices American or
　Provolone cheese

3 eggs, separated
½ cup flour
¾ cup sour cream
Salt and pepper to taste
Chopped parsley

Cook, drain and crumble bacon. Form a crust in 12x9-inch pan from un-folded dough. Sprinkle bacon over dough. Place tomatoes on top, cover with cheese slices. Beat egg whites until stiff in mixing bowl. Combine egg yolks, sour cream, flour and seasonings in separate bowl. Fold egg whites into yolk mixture. Pour over cheese. Sprinkle with parsley. Bake at 350 degrees for 35 to 40 minutes. Serves 6. *An easy brunch menu!*

BEER CHEESE FONDUE

¾ cup beer
2 cups Swiss cheese
1 cup Cheddar cheese

1 tablespoon all-purpose flour
Dash hot pepper sauce
Cubed bagels

Heat beer slowly. Coat cheese with flour. Gradually add to beer until thickened. Spear bagels and dip into sauce. Yields about 4 cups.

Trudy Jarret
Jax Beach, Florida

CHEDDAR PUFF

8 slices buttered bread with 3
　tablespoons butter
2 cups grated sharp cheddar
　cheese
4 eggs

2½ cups half and half
2 tablespoons Dijon mustard
1 teaspoon Worcestershire sauce
Salt and Pepper

Mix eggs, milk, mustard, Worcestershire sauce. Cube bread. Alternate layers of bread and cheese. Pour over milk mixture. Press cubes into milk mixture so all is coated. Refrigerate overnight or at least 4 hours. Bake uncovered until browned. *Nice accompaniment with ham or meat-loaf.* Serves 8 to 12.

Liz Mauceri
Southampton, New York

HAM AND CHEESE BAKE

16 slices day old bread (crusts cut off)
16 slices ham
16 slices cheese (Swiss and/or American)
6 eggs beaten
3 cups milk
½ teaspoon onion salt
¼ teaspoon dried mustard
½ cup melted butter
3 cups crushed corn flakes

Grease 9x12-inch baking dish with butter. Layer in following order: bread, ham, cheese, bread, ham, cheese. Pour mixture of eggs, milk and seasonings over layers. Refrigerate overnight. Heat oven to 400 degrees. Sprinkle corn flakes mixed with melted butter over top. Cook for 40 minutes. Serves 8. *Wonderful for brunch-served with fruit compote.*

Dorothy Mikus
Cranford, New Jersey

SAUSAGE STRATA

6 slices of bread
1 pound hot sausage, ground
1 cup grated sharp cheese
4 eggs
1 tablespoon prepared mustard
1 teaspoon Worcestershire sauce
1¼ cups milk
Dash of nutmeg

Remove crusts from bread and line rectangular pan. Fry and drain sausage. Put on bread layer. Sprinkle cheese over sausage. Beat together eggs, mustard, Worcestershire sauce, milk, and nutmeg. Pour over the bread, meat and cheese. Refrigerate overnight. Bake at 350 degrees for 30 minutes. Serves 4 to 6.

Peggy Settle (Sue Leaming)

ASPARAGUS OMELETTE

1 cup cooked asparagus, cut up
Oil
3 eggs beaten with salt and

pepper
3 tablespoons grated Italian
cheese

In medium size skillet, spray with Pam and add some oil to fill bottom of pan. Spread out and saute asparagus. Add egg mixture to make omelette. Flip over when done. Serves 4.

Jaye Guarino
Jax Beach, Florida

BEECHMONT SHIRRED EGGS

8 bread baskets

Bread Baskets
Cut crust from 8 bread slices. Roll slices flat with rolling pin. Butter one side and form, buttered side down, into a muffin tin. Bake at 325 degrees for 10 minutes. Remove and store in plastic bags in refrigerator or freezer.

Baked Eggs
8 bread baskets
8 thin slices of ham or smoked
   turkey
8 ounces shredded Cheddar
   cheese

8 eggs
Butter

Cut ham or turkey into rounds to fit in bread baskets (a small cookie cutter works well). Place bread basket into muffin tin. Put ham or turkey into bread basket and sprinkle with shredded cheese. Carefully crack an egg into basket. Top with shredded cheese and dot with butter. Bake at 325 degrees for 15 minutes (until egg white is set). Serves 8. *This recipe can easily be expanded or reduced.*

Beechmont Inn
Hanover, Pennsylvania

BLEU CHEESE DEVILED EGGS

12 hard cooked eggs
½ cup crumbled bleu cheese

½ cup sour cream
1 teaspoon vinegar

Halve eggs and remove yolk. Mash yolk with cheese and add sour cream and vinegar. Refill egg whites with mixture. Put 2 halves together. Cover with plastic wrap and refrigerate. (If desired, use 1 cup of egg yolk mixture to fill pastry tube. Squeeze a frill of egg mixture around egg where halves are together. Garnish with small piece of pimiento.) Yield 2 dozen halves.

Mary Kosak

CANADIAN BACONED EGGS

8 slices Canadian bacon
1 cup grated Swiss cheese
8 eggs

1 pint sour cream
4 English muffins (toasted)

Line casserole with Canadian bacon. Sprinkle Swiss cheese over bacon. Place a whole egg over each slice of bacon and cover yolk with sour cream. Sprinkle with paprika and bake at 325 degrees for 20 minutes. Serve on English muffin. Serves 4.

Mary LaBrecque Snyder, The Manor House

GOVERNOR'S EGG CASSEROLE

½ cup chopped onion
2 tablespoons butter
2 tablespoons flour
1¼ cup milk
1½ cups crushed potato chips

1 cup shredded sharp cheese
6 hard cooked eggs, sliced
10 to 12 slices cooked bacon,
   crumbled

Cook onion in butter until tender. Blend in flour and milk. Cook until thick, stirring constantly. Add cheese and stir until melted. In 9x6-inch casserole, layer ½ of eggs, ½ of cheese sauce, ½ of chips, ½ of bacon. Repeat. Bake at 350 degrees for 30 minutes. Serves 4. *This was served at the Kentucky's Derby Day Breakfast.*

Betty Deal
Medford, New Jersey

OVEN OMELETTE BRUNCH

¼ cup margarine
18 eggs
1 cup sour cream

1 cup milk
2 teaspoon salt
1 cup grated sharp cheese

Melt margarine in 13x9-inch baking dish in a 350 degree oven. Tilt to cover the bottom. With an electric mixer, beat eggs, sour cream, milk and salt. Stir in cheese. Pour into baking dish. Bake until set (approximately 45 minutes). Serves 12.

Diane Coldren

SCOTCH EGGS
Old English Recipe

6 hard boiled eggs, peeled
1 pound sausage
¼ teaspoon grated nutmeg
¼ teaspoon basil

¼ teaspoon marjoram
Freshly ground pepper
1 egg, beaten
4 ounces bread crumbs

Mix sausage and herbs thoroughly. Using wet hands, form a coating for each egg out of the sausage mix. Roll covered eggs in beaten egg and then bread crumbs. Heat oil in deep pan. When oil starts to smoke, add three eggs. Fry for 5 to 6 minutes, turning to brown evenly. Remove and drain on paper towel. Repeat. Cool and serve cut in half. Serves 6. *Can be made ahead for brunch, snacks and picnics.*

Helen Taylor

OEUFS BERCY

Eggs
12 eggs, hard boiled, shelled, and
   split in half lengthwise

Remove yolks and mash in a bowl.

Sauce 1
4 tablespoons butter
½ cup shallots, minced finely
½ cup finely chopped onion
1 cup dry white wine

1 cup chicken stock
½ teaspoon salt
White pepper

Sauce 1
Melt butter in saucepan. Add shallots and onions. Saute until transparent.
Add wine, chicken stock, salt and pepper. Bring to a boil and simmer until
liquid reduces to ½ volume.

Sauce 2
4 tablespoons butter
4 tablespoons flour

2 cups milk or half-and-half or
   light cream

Sauce 2
Melt butter in saucepan. Add flour and whisk over heat for two minutes.
While whisking, add milk or half-and-half or light cream. Bring to a boil,
whisking the entire time. Remove from heat. Slowly whisk Sauce 1 into this
mixture. Set aside.

Egg Yolk Stuffing
12 hard boiled egg yolks mashed
8 tablespoons softened butter
2 tablespoons Dijon mustard
2 teaspoons tomato paste
2 tablespoons bread crumbs
2 tablespoons Parmesan cheese

¼ pound ham, finely chopped
Juice of ½ lemon
2 garlic cloves, finely chopped
1 tablespoons parsley
Salt and pepper to taste

Egg Yolk Stuffing
Mix softened butter into mashed egg yolks. Add rest of stuffing ingredients and mix well.

To Assemble

Place hard boiled egg whites into a buttered au gratin pan and stuff with egg yolk stuffing. Mound stuffing high in egg white. Gently nap Bercy sauce (Sauce 1 and 2) over eggs. Sprinkle with Parmesan cheese and parsley. Bake at 375 for 10 to 15 minutes until hot and bubbly. Yields 2 dozen halves.

Bonita Wolchko-Rivera
Bryn Athyn, Pennsylvania

CHIPPED BEEF CASSEROLE

1 can mushroom soup
1 cup milk
6 ounces sharp cheese, shredded
3 tablespoons minced onions

1 cup uncooked elbow macaroni
¼ pound dried beef, rinsed, dried
   and cut into bite-size pieces
2 hard boiled eggs, sliced

Mix soup and milk well. Stir in cheese and onion. Fold in macaroni, dried beef, and eggs. Turn into a buttered 1½ quarts baking dish. Store covered in refrigerator at least 4 hours or overnight. Bake uncovered 1 hour at 350 degrees. Serves 4 to 6.

Sue Leaming

HUNGARIAN NOODLES

6 whole chicken breasts
1 pound fine noodles (vermicelli)
4 cups ricotta cheese
4 cups sour cream
1 cup minced onion
4 cloves garlic, minced

4 dashes hot pepper sauce
4 tablespoons poppy seeds
2 teaspoons salt
2 teaspoon pepper
2 tablespoons paprika
1 to 1½ cups Parmesan cheese

Cover breasts with water and cook. Skin, bone and chunk up chicken. Save broth. Cook noodles in broth and drain. Combine ricotta cheese, sour cream, onion, garlic, Tabasco, poppy seeds, salt and pepper. Mix combined ingredients with noodles and chicken chunks. Put in 13x9-inch greased pan. Top with Parmesan cheese and paprika. Bake at 350 degrees for 30 minutes. Serves 6 to 8.

Lynda Leaming
Orange, California

MATCHLESS MACARONI SALAD

1 (8-ounce) package shell
  macaroni
2 to 3 cups seedless green grapes,
  halved
1 (8-ounce) can pitted ripe olives,
  drained and halved
¾ cup chopped green onions

2 to 3 ounces bleu cheese,
  crumbled
Salt and pepper to taste
¼ teaspoon garlic powder
3 tablespoons fresh lemon juice
1 cup mayonnaise

Cook macaroni according to package directions. Drain. Combine hot macaroni with grapes, olives, onions, cheese, salt, pepper and garlic powder. Mix lemon juice and mayonnaise until smooth. Combine macaroni and mayonnaise until evenly mixed. Refrigerate covered several hours or overnight. Add more mayonnaise if desired before serving. Serves 8 to 12.

Sally Sachs

CREAMY MACARONI AND CHEESE

2 cups elbow macaroni, uncooked
3 tablespoons butter
2½ cups milk
½ teaspoon salt
Pepper (optional)

2½ cups sharp Cheddar cheese,
  shredded
½ cup shredded mozzerella cheese
½ cup Parmesan cheese
Paprika

Cook macaroni according to package directions, drain. Melt butter and blend in flour. Gradually add milk, cooking and stirring until Mixture thickens. Add salt, pepper, Cheddar and mozzarella cheese, stirring until cheese is melted. Combine sauce with cooked macaroni and mix well. Turn into a greased casserole. Sprinkle with Parmesan cheese and paprika. Bake at 30 degrees for 40 minutes. Serves 8.

Loretta Baver
Pennsburg, Pennsylvania

GREEN NOODLES
A Food Procesor Recipe

2½ cups tightly packed torn
    spinach leaves
¼ cup water

2 eggs
1 teaspoon salt
2½ cups flour

In covered pan, cook spinach in water until tender. Cool, but do not drain. Place steel blade in work bowl of food processor. Add drained spinach, eggs, and salt. Process intil smooth. Add flour and process until ball forms. On floured surface, roll half the dough at a time into a 12x15-inch rectangle. Let stand for 20 minutes. Roll up loosely. Slice ¼-inch wide strips and unroll. Cut into desired length. Spread onto racks and dry 2 hours. Cook uncovered in boiling, salted water for 10 to 15 minutes. If not cooking immediately store covered in refrigerator. Yields 7 cups. *This is a very easy recipe that can be made ahead.*

Christi Igoe
Seaville, New Jersey

NORFOLK NOODLES

12 ounces wide noodles
1 cup fresh parsley, chopped
1 pint carton large curd cottage
    cheese
1 pint carton sour cream
1 tablespoon Worcestershire
    sauce

Dash of hot pepper sauce
1 bunch green onion with tops
    chopped
½ cup grated sharp cheese
½ teaspoon paprika

Boil noodles according to directions on the package. Drain white noodles (still hot), mix in all the ingredients except cheese and paprika. Place in shallow baking dish. Refrigerate. When ready to bake, top with cheese and paprika. Place in 350 degree oven, uncovered, for 40 minutes or until cheese is melted. Serves 8.

Joan Warner

GARDEN PASTA SALAD

2 cups broccoli florets, cooked
1 cup pinwheel macaroni, cooked
8 ounces natural Cheddar cheese
2 medium tomatoes, cut into small pieces
½ cup chopped walnuts
1 teaspoon dried basil
¼ cup chopped parsley
¾ cup French dressing

Toss all ingredients together and cool before serving. Serves 4.

Mary Kosak

PASTA SALAD

1 pound linguini
1 (1-pound) can artichoke hearts, drained, patted dry
½ cup sliced black pitted olives
¼ cup olive oil
3 tablespoons fresh lemon juice
2 garlic cloves, minced
⅛ teaspoon dried red chili
Fresh ground pepper
Salt

Cook linguini and drain well, set aside. Combine other ingredients and mix well. Add linguini and let stand 1 hour at room temperature. Make sure all strands are covered. If you double recipe, do not double olive oil. Serves 4 to 6.

Betty Deal
Medford, New Jersey

PASTA SALAD

1 pound cooked rotini (swirls) pasta
1 bottle Italian salad dressing
1 bottle Salad Supreme spice
1 tomato, diced
1 onion, diced
1 green pepper, diced

Toss all ingredients and serve cold. Serves 4 to 6. *This recipe was given to me by my best friend Leslie Fleishner from Pittsburgh, Pennsylvania. My children all enjoy making this, even my son at college.*

Donna Wilson
Ocean City, New Jersey

PASTA PRIMAVERA

1 bunch broccoli, florets only
1 bunch asparagus, tips only
  (optional)
1 small zucchini, sliced
1 yellow squash, sliced
1 cup cut green beans
½ cup peas
1 pound vermicelli, cooked AL
  DENTE
1 cup thinly sliced mushrooms
2 cloves garlic, minced

1 bunch green onions, chopped
3 tablespoons butter
2 cups cherry tomatoes, cut in
  halves
¼ cup chopped parsley
2 tablespoons basil
¼ cup butter
3 tablespoons chicken broth
¾ cup heavy whipping cream
¾ cup fresh Parmesan cheese
Salt and pepper to taste

Cook each vegetable separately in boiling water until tender, but crisp. Rinse in cold water and drain well. (This part may be done ahead, refrigerating vegetables). Place cooked vegetables in a large bowl. In a skillet, saute mushrooms, onions and garlic in 2 tablespoons butter 2 minutes. Add tomatoes and cook another minute, gently stirring. Toss gently into bowl or vegetables, adding basil and parsley. In a large pan, melt ¼ cup butter. Add chicken broth, cream, cheese and salt and pepper. Stir until smooth. DO NOT BOIL. Add vegetables to heat through, then cooked pasta. Serves 6 to 4.

SPAGHETTI ALLA CARBONARA

1 pound bacon
4 large onions
2 cups dry white wine
12 eggs, beaten
2 cups grated Parmesan cheese
1 teaspoon freshly ground pepper

2 pound spaghetti or linguini (add
  2 to 3 tablespoons oil to boiling
  water)
¼ to ½ cup heavy whipping
  cream

Boil water for spaghetti. Cook bacon until lightly brown. Remove bacon and saute onion in bacon drippings until translucent. Cook bacon and return it to skillet and add wine. Simmer until liquid thickens. Beat eggs and add cheese and pepper in a large bowl. Cook spaghetti until AL DENTE. Pour hot spaghetti, drained, into egg mixture. Mix quickly and thoroughly. Add whipping cream to wet mixture. Pour bacon sauce over spaghetti. Mix all together and serve immediately. If mixture seems dry, add a little more cream. Serves 12.

Karen Hallberg
Wilmington, Delaware

SPAGHETTI ALA VENITA

6 medium or 1 (27 to 29-ounce)
  can tomatoes
8 ounces sharp Cheddar cheese
4 ounces heavy cream

¼ cup butter
1 pound spaghetti
Salt and pepper to taste (use
  fresh ground or coarse pepper)

While spaghetti is cooking heat butter and cream. Grate cheese. Combine cream and cheese, heat to melt cheese. Add tomatoes. Heat through. Toss cheese mixture with spaghetti. Salt and pepper to taste. Serves 4. *My Mother's Friday night supper.*

S. James Semple, Victorian Motel

SPAGHETTI SUPERB

2 tablespoons olive oil
4 cloves garlic, minced
1 green pepper, chopped
1 pound fresh mushrooms, sliced
1 pound hot sausage
1 pound ground chuck
1 (32-ounce) can Italian plum
  tomatoes (with basil if
  available)

2 (6-ounce) can tomato paste
2 tablespoons minced parsley
1 teaspoon oregano
1 tablespoon salt
1 teaspoon pepper
¾ cup red wine
1 pound spaghetti

In oil saute garlic, green pepper, onion and mushrooms. Cook sausage and ground chuck until browned, then drain. Add meats to vegetables and add remaining ingredients except spaghetti. Cover and simmer 2 hours. Serves 6 to 8.

Walter Sachs, Jr.

Breads

The Richard Ludlam House circa 1875

Originally on the corner of Ocean and Columbia, this house is
one of the few survivors on its block of the 1878 fire. It was
moved to its present location in 1907. The mansard roof and the
hyphenated palladian window in the front of the house are two
most noteworthy features.

QUICK AND EASY BANANA BREAD

1 cup sugar
1 cup soft butter
6 ripe bananas (mashed-3 cups)
4 eggs, beaten

2½ cups cake flour
2 teaspoons baking soda
1 teaspoon salt

Cream together sugar and butter with electric beater. Mix together bananas and eggs. Add to above until well mixed. Sift together flour, baking soda, salt. Blend with wet mixture. Lightly grease 2 loaf pans. Pour mixture evenly between the two. Bake at 350 degrees 45 to 60 minutes. Cool 10 minutes and remove from pans. Yields 2 loaves.

Arlene Fornabaio

(EASY) BEER BREAD

2 cups self-rising flour
3 tablespoons sugar

1 (12-ounce) can beer
1 tablespoon melted butter

Combine flour, sugar and beer until moistened. Pour into greased loaf pan. Bake at 375 degrees for 30 minutes or until done. Brush with melted butter. Remove from pan. Yields 1 loaf.

Julie Merson

BLUEBERRY BREAD

2 eggs
1 cup sugar
1 cup milk
¼ cup melted butter

3 cups flour
1 teaspoon salt
4 teaspoons baking powder
2 cups blueberries

Beat eggs and sugar. Add milk and butter. Add dry ingredients and mix until moistened. Toss blueberries in a little flour and stir in. Pour into greased bread pans. Bake at 350 degrees for 30 to 40 minutes. Yields 2 small loaves or 4 mini loaves.

Julie Merson

COCONUT BREAD

1 cup shortening
2 cups sugar
5 eggs
2 cups flour
1 teaspoon salt
1 teaspoon baking powder

1 cup buttermilk
1⅓ cups (3½-ounces) coconut
1 tablespoon coconut extract
¼ cup water
1 teaspoon coconut extract
½ cup sugar

Cream shortening, sugar and eggs, beat well. Sift flour, salt, baking powder. Add dry ingredients to egg mixture, alternating with buttermilk. Add coconut and 1 tablespoon extract. Grease and flour 3 small loaf pans to within 1 inch of top. Bake at 350 degrees for 50 to 60 minutes. Remove from oven. Combine ¼ cup water, 1 teaspoon extract and ½ cup sugar, boil for 2 minutes. Puncture top of bread with fork and pour on glaze. Cool. Yields 3 loaves. *I use this recipe as a dessert and think it is excellent for that.*

Mrs. Jane B. Runyan
York, Pennsylvania

CRANBERRY NUT BREAD

2 cups flour
½ teaspoon salt
½ teaspoon baking powder
½ teaspoon baking soda
1 cup sugar
2 tablespoons shortening, melted

1 egg, beaten
1 cup pecans, chopped
1 cup raw cranberries
Boiling water
1 orange

Sift flour, salt, soda, powder and sugar. Set aside. Using food processor or blender, process whole orange including rind, to form liquid. Place in 1 cup measuring cup, add melted shortening and enough boiling water to make 1 cup. Add the orange liquid to beaten egg, then add to dry ingredients. Fold in pecans and cranberries. Bake in greased 9x5-inch loaf pan at 325 degrees for 1 hour to 1 hour 15 minutes. Yields 1 loaf.

Mary Suzanne Roehm
Grosse Pointe, Michigan

GRANOLA MUFFINS

1 cup granola
½ cup snipped dried apricots
½ cup boiling water
1¾ cups flour
½ cup sugar

½ cup chopped walnuts
1 tablespoon baking powder
1 beaten egg
⅔ cup milk
½ cup oil

Combine granola, apricots and boiling water; set aside. In mixing bowl, stir egg, milk and oil into apricot mixture. Add all at once to flour mixture. Stir just until moistened (batter should be lumpy). Spoon into greased or paper bake cup lined muffin cups. Bake in 375 degree oven 20 to 25 minutes. Yields 18.

Christy Igoe
Seaville, New Jersey

HERB BREAD

2 cups flour
⅓ cup sugar
½ teaspoon salt
1½ teaspoons baking powder
½ teaspoon soda
¼ teaspoon marjoram

¼ teaspoon oregano
½ teaspoon basil
A pinch of thyme
1 egg, lighly beaten
¼ to ⅔ cup buttermilk
1 tablespoon melted butter

Sift flour, sugar, salt, baking powder and soda into a bowl. Add herbs and mix thoroughly. In a separate bowl, beat the egg. Add buttermilk and butter. Stir into dry ingredients, mix until moistened throughout. Add more milk if needed to make the dough cling together. Turn onto a floured board and knead until it handles well. Juggle it until you have a good round ball. Place in a well buttered pan or cake tin. Cut a cross in the top. This keeps the devil out. Bake at 375 degrees for 40 minutes. Yields 1 loaf. *Good served warm with sweet butter. Variations:* Use raisins or nuts - Instead of herbs use 1 tablespoon of dill seeds and a sprinkling of dillweed.

Ann Miller

PUMPKIN BREAD

Dry

3½ cups flour	½ teaspoon salt
2 teaspoons baking soda	3 teaspoons cinnamon
3 teaspoons nutmeg	1 cup walnuts (chopped)

Wet

2 cups pumpkin	⅔ cup water
3 cups sugar	1 cup oil
4 beaten eggs	

Mix all dry ingredients together. Make a well and put in wet ingredients which have already been mixed thoroughly. Mix again thoroughly. Bake at 350 degrees for 1 hour or less. Yields 3 loaves (9x5x3-inch). *Serves 12 slices per loaf. Freezes well.*

M. Edna Andrus
Haddon Township, New Jersey

SHORTCUT MONKEY BREAD

¾ cup granulated sugar	1 cup chopped walnuts or pecans
1 teaspoon ground cinnamon	
3 cans refrigerated biscuits (8 to 10 biscuits each)	

Topping

½ cup butter	1 teaspoon vanilla
1 cup brown sugar	

Preheat oven to 350 degrees. Combine granulated sugar and cinnamon in a paper bag, shaking to mix well. Cut biscuits into quarters. Add chopped nuts and pieces of biscuit dough to bag and shake to coat well. Empty contents of bag into a thoroughly buttered tube pan (solid pan only) or bundt pan, arranging biscuit pieces neatly. Prepare topping by melting to boiling. Remove and pour hot topping over biscuits. Bake at 350 degrees for 30 to 35 minutes until done. Invert on serving board, waxed paper, etc. and serve warm. Yields 1 loaf. *Taken from a recent Philadelphia Inquirer. Delicious and reheats well.*

Laura G. Wagar

IRISH SODA BREAD

3½ cups sifted flour
½ cup sugar
1 teaspoon salt
½ teaspoon baking soda

½ teaspoon baking powder
2 eggs lightly beaten
1 pint sour cream
1 cup raisins

Mix dry ingredients, then fold in beaten eggs and sour cream. Stir in raisins, mold into round loaf. Grease a 2½-quart glass casserole and fill with batter. Sprinkle loaf with flour, cut a cross in top with knife. Bake at 325 degrees for 1 hour to 1 hour 15 minutes. Yields 1 loaf. *Remove from casserole when baked. Best served warm.*

Donna Misner, Abigail Adams Bed and Breakfast

QUICK SOUR CREAM ROLLS

2 cups buttermilk biscuit mix
6 tablespoons butter or margarine

1 cup sour cream

Melt butter and stir well into biscuit mix. Add sour cream. Grease three miniature muffin tins. Fill each cup about ⅔ full by dropping mixture using 2 spoons in portions about the size of a walnut into each. Bake at 375 degrees about 8 to 10 minutes or until golden brown. Turn onto cake rack to cool or serve immediately. Yields 3 dozen. *These rolls are rich and do not need any additional buttering. Tops will not be smooth. Can be frozen. Large muffin pans not recommended.*

Mary Suzanne Roehm
Grosse Pointe, Michigan

SOUTHERN SPOON BREAD

2½ cups milk, scalded
1 cup sifted cornmeal (scant if
   yellow. Water ground white
   meal is very good)

1½ tablespoons butter
4 eggs, separated
1 teaspoon baking powder
1 teaspoon salt

Add scalded milk to cornmeal. Add salt, cook, stirring constantly until thick like mush. Stir in butter. Cool slightly. Beat egg yolks, add to above with baking powder. Mix well. Fold in stiffly beaten egg whites. Turn into hot buttered casserole. Bake at 375 degrees for ½ hour or until firm and brown. Serve immediately. Serves 6. *I understand this was Wally Simpson's recipe (Duchess of Windsor), taken from a Baltimore newspaper. It was given to me by a friend in Honolulu in 1946. I've passed it along to many friends. It's been "published" many times.*

Nell Pearson
Silver Spring, Maryland

SWEET POTATO MUFFINS

½ cup butter
1¼ cups sugar
2 eggs
1¼ cups canned sweet potatoes,
   mashed
1½ cups flour
2 teaspoons baking powder

¼ teaspoon salt
1 teaspoon cinnamon
¼ teaspoon nutmeg
1 cup milk
¼ cup pecans or walnuts, chopped
½ cup raisins, chopped

Preheat oven to 400 degrees. Grease 1½-inch muffin tins. Cream the butter and sugar. Add the eggs and mix well. Blend in the sweet potatoes. Sift the flour with baking powder, salt, cinnamon and nutmeg. Add alternately with the milk. Do not overmix. Fold in nuts and raisins. Fill the greased muffin tins ⅔ full. Bake at 400 degrees for 25 minutes. Yields 6 dozen mini muffins. *Muffins can be frozen and reheated.*

Elizabeth von Schlichten

SWEET POTATO BREAD

2 cups flour
2½ teaspoons baking powder
½ teaspoon salt
¼ teaspoon allspice
¼ teaspoon nutmeg
1 cup cooked, mashed sweet
   potatoes

½ cup packed brown sugar
¼ cup melted unsalted margarine
¼ cup chopped pecans
6 tablespoons skim milk
2 teaspoons orange rind
2 eggs

Combine first 5 ingredients in large bowl. Set aside. Combine potatoes, sugar, margarine, milk, eggs, orange rind and nuts. Beat well. Add to dry ingredients, stirring only until moistened. Because sweet potatoes vary so widely, I add more milk now if batter seems too thick. Pour batter into 9x5x3-inch loaf pan coated with cooking spray. Bake at 350 degrees for 45 minutes or until tests done. Cool in pan 10 minutes. Remove and cool completely. Yields 18 slices. *125 calories per slice!*

Donna Gaver Shank
Dover, Delaware

QUICK WHOLE WHEAT BREAD

¼ cup honey
¼ cup brown sugar
¾ cup milk
¾ cup cold water
2 cups whole wheat flour

1 cup flour
1¾ teaspoons baking powder
1 teaspoon salt
¾ teaspoon baking soda

Dissolve honey and sugar in milk and water. Stir in dry ingredients until moistened. Bake in a well-greased 9x5x4-inch bread pan at 275 degrees for 1½ hours or until pick comes out clean. Remove from pan. Cool. Wrap in foil while slightly warm. Refrigerate. Yields 1 loaf. *Nuts, oatmeal, raisins, dates may be added. Can replace white flour with branflakes, wheat germ, soy or rye.*

Julie Merson

YOGURT BREAD

1 cup sugar
2 cups flour
1 teaspoon baking soda
2 teaspoons baking powder
¼ cup butter or margarine

1 egg
1 cup plain yogurt
2 tablespoons sugar
2 tablespoons cinnamon

Mix and sift sugar, flour, baking soda and baking powder. Cut in butter with pastry blender or 2 knives. Add egg and yogurt and beat thoroughly. Pour ½ of batter into greased loaf pan, sprinkle with ½ of sugar and cinnamon mixture. Add remaining batter and sprinkle with rest of sugar and cinnamon mixture. Bake at 350 degrees for 40 to 50 minutes. Yield 1 loaf. *Family recipe, freezes well.*

Florence and Joanne Heal

FRENCH TOAST

1 cup flour
1 egg
½ tablespoon baking powder
1 tablespoon sugar
½ cup milk

¼ tablespoon vanilla
Solid shortening
Stale or day old bread-sliced
    diagonally

Mix first six ingredients into a batter. Dip bread in batter. Fry in hot shortening, brown both sides. Sprinkle with powdered sugar. Serves 4. *Serve with a variety of jellies or jams.*

Darlene Orminski

COLVMNS PEACH TOAST

3 eggs
3 tablespoons peach preserves
¾ cup half and half
6 slices French bread ½-inch thick
⅓ cup peach preserves

½ cup butter, softened
2 fresh peaches
Powdered sugar
Toasted almonds

In small bowl beat eggs and 3 tablespoons peach preserves with whisk until blended. Beat in half and half. Place single layer of bread in an 11x7-inch baking dish. Pour egg mixture over bread. Cover and refrigerate overnight. In a small bowl beat ⅓ cup peach preserves and 4 tablespoons butter until fluffy. Set aside in refrigerator. In morning add 2 tablespoons butter to a large skillet. Add 3 slices of bread, cook over medium heat until browned, turning once. Keep warm while repeating with other 3 slices. Serve topped with 1 teaspoon peach butter (above) and fresh peach slices. Sprinkle with toasted almonds and powdered sugar. Serves 4 to 6. *Used at Colvmns By The Sea on special occasions, serve with ham slices.*

Barry Rein and Cathy Rein, COLVMNS by the Sea

SOUR CREAM WAFFLES

3 eggs
¾ cup milk
½ cup butter
¾ cup sour cream

1½ cups flour
2 teaspoons baking powder
½ teaspoon baking soda
l tablespoon sugar

Separate eggs and beat the yolks in a bowl. Beat in milk, melted butter and sour cream. Set aside. combine and sift together flour, baking powder, baking soda and sugar. Add to the wet mixture and beat well. Beat the egg whites until stiff and carefully fold into batter. Bake in a hot waffle iron and serve with desired topping. Serves 8. *I freeze these then pop in toaster either for breakfast or with ice cream.*

Christy Igoe
Seaville, New Jersey

POP PANCAKES

1 cup pancake mix   2 tablespoons melted butter
1 egg
1 bottle lemon-lime carbonated
  soda

Combine all ingredients well. Use just enough lemon-lime soda (approximately 8 ounces). Bake on hot buttered griddle for about 1½ minutes or until goden brown. Then turn and bake on other side. Yield 8 to 12 pancakes.
Note: You may substitute gingerale, root beer or cola for lemon-lime soda.

Turdy Jarret
Jax Beach, Florida

Entrees

John B. McCreary House 1869
Corner of Columbia and Guerney

Of exceptional interest is this house of unusual grace and
beauty. It is easily identified by its elaborate crowning touch.
A design by S. D. Button for a wealthy coal baron from Pennsylvania produced this marvelous Gothic Revival with its 60
foot tower. Gingerbread abounds in lace trim which differ on
each side of the house.

BAKED FLOUNDER

1½ pounds flounder fillets
1½ cups milk
1 teaspoon salt
3 tablespoons butter

3 tablespoons flour
¼ pound cheese, grated
2 tablespoons Worcestershire
    sauce or lemon juice

Roll fillets and fasten with toothpickes. Place in baking dish and add milk and salt. Bake at 375 degrees for 30 to 40 minutes. Make white sauce by melting butter in saucepan, adding flour and stirring until smooth. Add milk from baked fish to sauce and continue to cook until thick and smooth. Fold in cheese and stir until melted. Add Worcestershire sauce or lemon juice. Pour over fish and lightly brown under broiler. Serves 4 to 6. *Good when served with rice, warm Italian bread and a salad.*

Virginia Morrow

BALTIMORE INN DEVILED CLAMS

1 dozen large clams, ground (save
    shells and juice)
3 tablespoons butter
3 tablespoons flour
A little milk
2 eggs, beaten

1 cup bread crumbs
1 tablespoon parsley
1 tablespoon celery leaves
½ teaspoon minced onion
Pinch of paprika

Bring clam juice to a boil and skim scum. Melt butter, stir in flour and add juice and enough milk to make two cups. Boil until thick (about ten minutes). Remove from stove and add clams, seasonings and crumbs. Fill scrubbed shells, sprinkle with paprika. Bake at 450 degrees for 20 minutes. Serves 6. *The Baltimore Inn stood on Jackson Street, Cape May, for years.*

Sally Hirsh

CLAM SAUCE

2 dozen cherrystone clams,
  shucked
3 cloves garlic, finely chopped
¾ cup olive oil
1 cup butter
½ cup parsley, finely chopped

1 teaspoon basil
½ teaspoon oregano
Dash of crushed red pepper
Dash of freshly ground black
  pepper

Drain clams, saving their liquor. Chop clams coarsely. Saute garlic in combined olive oil and butter for 5 minutes. Add the clams, their liquor and seasonings. Simmer for 20 minutes, stirring occasionally. Yields about 6 cups. *To make red clam sauce, add 2 cups canned tomato puree when adding the clams.*

Deborah B. Guilloz
Southampton, New York

CRAB AND RICE RAMEKINS

1 cup cooked rice
1 cup crabmeat
1 cup medium cream sauce
1 teaspoon salt
½ teaspoon paprika
½ teaspoon Worcestershire sauce

1 teaspoon prepared mustard
½ teaspoon grated onion
Bread crumbs
Butter
Grated cheese

Preheat oven to 400 degrees. Combine crab and rice. Add cream sauce and seasonings and mix. Butter ramekins (may use individual white scallop shells) and fill with mixture. Cover with bread crumbs. Dot with butter. Sprinkle with cheese. Bake for 30 minutes, until brown. Serves 4.

Debra Chapman

CRAB IMPERIAL

1 pound lump crabmeat
½ cup mayonnaise
1 egg
1 teaspoon dry mustard

½ teaspoon salt
⅛ teaspoon white pepper
Dash of paprika

Pick through crabmeat to remove shell. Mix mayonnaise with remaining ingredients, blend in crabmeat and spoon into individual casseroles. Top with paprika. Bake at 350 degrees oven for 15 minutes. Serves 4.

Craig Smith

CLASSIC CRAB IMPERIAL

4 tablespoons butter
2 tablespoons flour
1 teaspoon salt
⅛ teaspoon pepper
1 teaspoon dry mustard
1 cup milk or light cream

½ small green pepper, minced
1 teaspoon Worcestershire sauce
1 pound crabmeat
2 hard boiled eggs, diced
  (optional)
Buttered bread crumbs

Make white sauce using first six ingredients. Add green pepper, Worcestershire sauce and crabmeat. Mix well, pour into buttered casserole and sprinkle diced eggs and bread crumbs over top. Bake at 400 degrees for 30 minutes until bubbly and brown. Serves 4. *The diced eggs are a nice touch for added flavor.*

Mrs. Gordon H. Baver

CRAB QUICHE

6 ounces crabmeat
1 cup shredded sharp American
  cheese
1 (3-ounce) package cream cheese,
  cut into ¼-inch cubes
¼ cup sliced green onion
1 (2-ounce) jar chopped pimiento

2 cups milk
Dash of nutmeg
1 cup buttermilk biscuit baking
  mix
4 eggs
¾ teaspoon salt

Heat oven to 400 degrees. Grease 10-inch pie plate. Mix crabmeat, cheeses, onions and pimiento in plate. Beat remaining ingredients until smooth (about 15 seconds in blender on high or 1 minute with hand beater). Pour into plate. Bake about 35 to 40 minutes until knife inserted in center comes out clean. Cool 5 minutes before serving. Serves 8. *Cheddar may be substituted in place of American cheese.*

Judith J. Carter
Audubon, New Jersey

DOWN JERSEY CLAM PIE

2 dozen clams, chopped (reserve
  juice)
1 medium can white potatoes,
  diced
2 ribs celery, cut in small pieces

2 carrots, cut in small pieces
1 small onion, diced
Two 9-inch frozen pie crusts,
  thawed

Combine all ingredients, except reserved juice, in pie shell. Cover with clam juice (can be thickened before adding, if desired). Add top pie crust. Bake at 350 degrees fo 40 to 45 minutes. Serves 4. *Oysters may be substituted.*

Mary Prouty
Barrington, New Jersey

ENGLISH FISH AND CHIPS

4 Idaho potatoes, peeled and cut
   into ½-inch strips
Oil
1½ pounds fish fillets, cut into
   1½-inch strips
Salt

1 cup flour, sifted
1 teaspoon baking powder
1 teaspoon salt
¾ cup milk
Cider vinegar

Soak potatoes in cold water for 30 minutes, drain and dry on paper towels. Heat oil, at least ½-inch deep in large skillet, and fry potatoes until golden brown (aobut 20 minutes). Place fried potaotes in pan lined with paper towels and keep warm in 250 degree oven. Sprinkle fish with salt. Mix flour, baking powder and salt. Add milk and egg, and beat until smooth. Dip fish into batter and drop carefully into hot oil. Fry about 3 minutes, turn and brown another 3 minutes. Drain and serve fish and chips hot, with cider vinegar. Serves 4.

Gloria Smith
Mantoloking, New Jersey

FISH FILLETS WITH MUSTARD-CAPER SAUCE

2 pounds fish fillets (flounder,
   sole)
1 cup dry white wine
2 tablespoons capers

1 tablespoon Dijon mustard
½ cup heavy cream
1½ tablespoons cornstarch
2 tablespoons water

Preheat oven to 400 degrees. Wash fillets and pat dry. Arrange in buttered baking dish. Pour wine over fillets, cover lightly with foil and bake for 10 minutes. Remove pan from oven and carefully pour poaching liquid into small saucepan. (Fish can be prepared up to this point and refrigerated). Reduce oven to 350 degrees. Add capers and mustard to poaching liquid. Bring to boil, lower heat and simmer for 1 minute. Stir cream into musard-caper mixture. Combine cornstarch with water and slowly add to sauce. Cook until slightly thickened. Spoon sauce over fish and bake for 10 minutes. Serve 6. *Delicious served with parsley rice and asparagus or broccoli.*

Laura G. Wagar

FISH CASSEROLE

½ pound each, shrimp, crab,
   scallops and monkfish or lobster
3 tablespoons butter
½ cup sherry

2 cans cream of mushroom soup
½ teaspoon dry mustard
½ teaspoon paprika
⅓ cup heavy or sour cream

Saute all fish in butter, drain if necessary. Add sherry and simmer 15 minutes. Add soup, mustard and paprika and simmmer 10 minutes. Add additional mushrooms if desired. Mix in cream, pour into casserole and bake at 350 degrees for 20 minutes. Serves 5 to 6. *May double ingredients and freeze before baking. Serve with rice.*

Jeannie Wood

E-Z FISH FLORENTINE

3 pounds fresh fillets, flounder or
   cod
3 teaspoons butter
3 tablespoons half and half

1 can cream of spinach soup
Dash of paprika
Lemon wedges

Place fish in glass baking dish and top with next three ingredients. Bake uncovered at 325 degrees for 20 to 30 minutes. Sprinkle with paprika for color and serve with lemon wedges. Serves 6.

Louise Krause

FLOUNDER IN FOIL

4 fillets of flounder
Butter
½ red onion, thinly sliced

1 lime, peeled and thinly sliced
1 tomato, chopped
Sprigs of thyme

Wash fillets and pat dry with paper towels. Cut 4 pieces of heavy aluminum foil about twice the size of each fillet and dot with butter. Sprinkle onion over the buttered areas and place fillets on top. Place remaining ingredients on fillets. Seal foil tightly with two folds to prevent leaks. Grill over hot coals 8 to 10 minutes. Serve each person an individual flounder in foil. Serves 4.

Donna G. Shank
Dover, Delaware

FLOUNDER IN SPINACH

1 cup sour cream
1 medium onion, chopped
1½ tablespoons flour
2 tablespoons lemon juice
1 teaspoon salt

2 packages frozen chopped
  spinach, cooked and drained
1 to 1½ pounds flounder fillets
¼ pound mushrooms, sliced
Paprika

Preheat oven to 375 degrees. Mix together first five ingredients. Add half of mixture to spinach and place in bottom of shallow 13x10-inch baking dish. Arrange fillets on top. Spread mushrooms over fillets and top with remaining sour cream mixture. Spinkle with paprika. Bake for 20 minutes. Serves 4 to 6.

Patricia Rafftesaeth

FLOUNDER PARMESAN

2 pounds flounder fillets
6 tablespoons grated Parmesan
  cheese
1 tablespoon grated oinion
1 cup buttermilk

1 tablespoon lemon juice
1½ teaspoons salt
Dash of hot pepper sauce
Paprika
Chopped fresh parsley

Arrange fish in single layer in baking dish. Mix remaining ingredients, except paprika and parsley. Spread mixture over fish, sprinkle with paprika. Bake at 350 degrees for 25 minutes. Garnish with parsley. Serves 6. *Great low-cal dish. 160 calories each!*

Trudy Jarret
Jax Beach, Florida

HERB DUMPLING ON BAKED CRAB

1 (7½ ounce) can King crab
¼ cup butter
¼ cup minced onion
½ cup diced celery
½ teaspoon salt
½ teaspoon dry mustard
½ teaspoon Worcestershire sauce
⅓ cup flour

1½ cups milk
1 cup Cheddar cheese
1 (16 ounce) can tomatoes, drained and chopped
1½ cups buttermilk biscuit baking mix
⅓ cup water or milk
¼ teaspoon each, thyme, basil and marjoram

To make crab cheese sauce
Drain and slice crab. Melt butter in sauce pan, add onion and celery and saute until tender. Stir in salt, mustard, Worcestershire sauce and flour. Gradually add milk, cooking over medium heat until thickened, stirring constantly. Remove from heat and stir in crab, grated cheese and tomatoes. Continue to stir until cheese is melted. Pour into 2 quart shallow baking dish.

To make herb dumplings
Combine baking mix with water and herbs, stirring until blended. Divide mixture into six portions and place on crab mixture. Bake at 375 degrees for 15 to 20 minutes or until biscuits are browned. Serves 6. *½ pound fresh or frozen crab, shrimp or combination of seafood may be substituted in place of canned crab.*

Doris Jarden

RIBBON OYSTER STEW

2 cans oyster stew
2 cans oysters
1 small can sliced mushrooms
2 cups crushed oyster crackers

Few drops hot pepper sauce
2 tablespoons parsley, chopped
2 tablespoons butter

Remove oysters from stew. Drain liquid from canned oysters and mushrooms. Put liquid into stew liquid. Heat to boiling. Stir in 1½ cups oyster crackers. Heat until thick. Add all oysters, mushrooms, and hot pepper sauce. Pour into oblong 12x8x2-inch casserole. Place remaining crackers on top. Spoon melted butter over stew. Add Parsley. Bake at 425 degrees for 10 minutes. Serves 6 to 8.

Jessie Lisk
Springfield, Pennsylvania

LOBSTER IN TOMATO SAUCE

6 (5-ounce) frozen rock lobster
   tails, unthawed
Or 3½ cups cut up cooked lobster
2 tablespoons butter or margarine
1½ cups finely chopped onion
1 clove garlic, finely chopped
1 (6-ounce) can tomato paste
¼ cup finely chopped parsley
1 teapoon dried thyme leaves
1 bay leaf, crumbled
1 teaspoon salt
¼ teaspoon pepper
1 cup dry white wine
¼ cup brandy (optional)

Cook lobster tails as package label directs; let cool. Remove meat from shells and cut into large chunks. In hot butter in large skillet, saute onion and garlic until golden about 5 minutes. Remove from heat. Stir in remaining ingredients except lobster; bring to boiling; reduce heat, simmer, covered about 15 minutes. Add lobster and gently heat for 5 minutes. Do not overheat, will toughen and shrink lobster. Serves 6. *Easy and elegant. Can be served over spaghetti, rice or noodles. Good with a watercress and endive salad and a nice French bread.*

Sally Sachs

POACHED FISH CREOLE

¼ cup minced onion
¼ cup diced green pepper
1 clove garlic, minced
1 (16-ounce) can tomatoes,
   undrained and coarsely chopped
2 teaspoons Worcestershire sauce
2 teaspoons red wine vinegar
½ teaspoon dried whole basil
¼ teaspoon pepper
Dash of hot sauce
1 pound fish fillets (flounder, sole,
   perch)

Coat skillet with cooking spray and place over medium heat until hot. Saute onion and green pepper until tender (4 to 5 minutes). Add remaining ingredients, except fillets, and bring to boil. Add fillets, spooning sauce on top. Cover, reduce heat and simmer 2 minutes. Uncover and simmer 10 additional minutes or until fillets flake easily with a fork. Serves 4.

Donna Shank
Dover, Delaware

OYSTER FRITTERS

1 cup flour
2 teaspoons baking powder
1 egg, beaten
1 tablespoon oil

¼ cup milk
1 cup chopped oysters
Additional oil for frying

Combine flour baking powder and set aside. Combine remaining ingredients and blend into flour mixture, stirring until just moistened (if too dry, add a little oyster juice). Drop by tablespoons into ¼-inch of hot oil. Fry until medium brown on each side. Drain well on paper towels. Yields about 16 fritters, to serve 4.

Evelyn M. Todd

SALMON STRUDEL

3 hard boiled eggs, chopped
2 onions, chopped
2 garlic cloves, finely minced
½ cup bread crumbs
1 teaspoon dry mustard
¼ teaspoon ground cardamom
  seed
¼ cup grated Parmesan cheese

½ teaspoon salt
½ teaspoon pepper
½ pound butter, melted
½ box filo dough
½ pound smoked or fresh poached
  salmon, cut in strips
1 cup sour cream
Fresh dill

Take three bowls. Put eggs in one. Mix garlic and onion in another bowl. In last bowl, mix next six ingredients and about 4 tablespoons of the melted butter to hold mixture together. Set aside. Place a dry Turkish towel on counter and cover with a dampened tea towel. Place one sheet of filo dough on top of tea towel and brush with butter. Place a second sheet on top and brush with butter. Sprinkle half of bread crumb mixture on layers of filo, then add half of the onion mixture and finally, half of the eggs. Add salmon and remaining ingredients. Dollop sour cream over entire surface and top with fresh dill. Fold each edge of filo over about 1½ inches, brush with melted butter and roll up strudel fashion using tea towel. Butter and bake at 375 degrees for 45 to 50 minutes on a jelly roll pan. Serves 6. *May be assembled and refrigerated in advance like brownies. May be assembled and refrigerated in advance.*

Bonita Wolchko Rivera

98

SCALLOPED OYSTERS

2 tablespoons chopped onion
½ cup butter
1 teaspoon celery salt
1 tablespoon lemon juice
½ teaspoon pepper

1 teaspoon Worcestershire sauce
1½ cups cracker crumbs
1 pint (2 dozen) medium oysters, drained
½ cup light cream

Saute onion in butter. Remove from heat and stir in remaining ingredients (except oysters and cream). In 2-quart casserole, layer a third of the crumbs, half of the oysters, another third of the crumbs, the second half of the oysters, and top with remaining crumbs. Pour sour cream over the casserole and bake at 350 degrees for 30 to 45 minutes or until brown. Serves 4 to 5. If doubling recipe, use 5 dozen oysters.

Barbara Jackson
Haddon Heights, New Jersey

SEAFOOD BROCHETTE

1 pound rockfish fillets, cut into 1-inch squares
1 (13½ ounce) can pineapple chunks, drained
½ pound mushrooms
1 green pepper, cut into 1 inch squares

½ pound cherry tomatoes
¼ cup oil
¼cup lemon juice
¼ cup parsley
¼ cup soy sauce
⅝ teaspoon salt
Dash of pepper

Place first five items in bowl. Combine oil, lemon juice, parsley, soy sauce, salt and pepper. Pour over mixture in bowl and let stand at least 30 minutes, stirring occasionally. Alternate on skewers and cook over grill, basting with sauce. Serves 4 to 6. May substitute any firm fish, such as shark, monkfish, or mahi-mahi.

Sally Brice-O'Hara

SEAFOOD NEWBURG

3 tablespoons flour
4 tablespoons butter
1 tablespoon paprika
1 teaspoon salt
Pinch of cayenne

2 cups heavy cream
⅔ cup sherry
2 cups (about 1 pound) shellfish, cooked

Make a light roux of flour and butter and simmer 5 minutes. Add spices and blend well. Stir in cream and simmer 15 minutes. Add sherry and simmer 5 minutes. Add shellfish and heat through. Serves 6. *Best if served with rice.*

SEAFOOD WITH CURRY SAUCE

4 tablespoons butter
2 tablespoons curry powder
3 tablespoons flour
1 cup chicken broth
1 cup light cream
Pinch of salt

Pinch of pepper
½ pound shrimp, cooked and peeled
½ pound crabmeat
½ pound lobster meat, cooked

Melt butter in saucepan, add curry powder and stir in flour until smooth. Add chicken broth, stir, then add cream, stirring constantly over low heat until thickened. Add salt and pepper to taste. Add seafood, mixing thoroughly, and pour into casserole. Bake in 350 degrees oven for about 15 minutes. Serves 4 to 6.

SEAFOOD RAREBIT SOUFFLE

1 can cream of shrimp soup
1 soup can of milk
4 eggs
¼ cup sherry
1 teaspoon dry mustard

Salt to taste
1 pound of fresh crab
8 slices of buttered white bread, quartered
4 cups grated Cheddar cheese

Combine soup, milk, eggs, sherry, mustard, salt, crab:; mix well. Arrange alternate layers of bread, cheese and crab mixture in buttered 1½-quart casserole. Refrigerate overnight. Bake at 350 degrees for 1 hour. Serve at once. Serves 6 to 8.

Denise Heckel

SEVICHE OF BAY SCALLOPS
WITH MIXED PEPPERS

2 pounds fresh bay scallops
1 cup freshly squeezed lime juice
½ cup olive oil
2 tablespoons chili paste or hot
 pepper sauce
1½ tablespoons fresh crushed
 black pepper
1½ tablespoons oregano

1½ tablespoons crushed coriander
½ tablespoon ground thyme
2 cloves garlic, minced
1 each green, red and yellow
 peppers, finely juilienned
1 medium tomato, diced
1 bunch green onions, sliced

Clean muscle from scallops. Place in glass dish with lime juice, cover and refrigerate for two hours (the acids of the lime juice act as the cooking agent in this procedure). Blend oil and spices. Toss prepped vegetables with this marinade, then mix thoroughly with scallops and juice. Seviche should remain refrigerated until served. Serves 8. *If scallops are not available, any meaty fish (such as snapper, monk fish, whitefish) may be substituted.*

The Pilot House Restaurant

SHRIMP CASSEROLE

⅓ cup finely chopped onion
1 or 2 cloves garlic, finely minced
2 tablespoons butter
2 pounds uncooked shrimp,
 shelled and deveined
1 cup uncooked rice
1 large can tomatoes
2 cups chicken bouillon or canned
 consomme

Bay leaf
3 tablespoons chopped parsley
½ teaspoon cloves
1 teaspoon chili powder
Dash of cayenne
1 tablespoon salt
⅛ teaspoon pepper

Brown onion and garlic in butter. Mix with the shrimp, rice, tomatoes and boullion and place in casserole. Add remaining seasonings. Cover tightly and bake for 1½ hours at 350 degrees. Serves 6. *If your guests are late, this holds another hour.*

Doris Jarden

SHRIMP AND ARTICHOKE HEARTS EN CASSEROLE

2 tablespoons butter
2½ tablespoons flour
½ teaspoon salt
¼ teaspoon pepper
⅛ teaspoon cayenne pepper
1 cup cream
1 tablespoon Worcestershire
   sauce
¼ cup dry sherry

1 (#2 can) whole artichoke
   hearts, drained
1 pound shrimp, cooked and
   peeled
½ pound mushrooms, coarsely
   sliced
2 tablespoons butter
¼ cup Parmesan cheese
Paprika

Make a medium thick cream sauce by melting first 2 tablespoons butter in saucepan, stirring in flour. When smooth, add salt, peppers and cream. cook, stirring constantly, until smooth. Add next ingredients, blend well and set aside. Quarter artichokes and arrange in a buttered casserole, then spread shrimp over them. Saute mushrooms in remaining butter for 6 to 7 minutes and layer over shrimp. Pour cream sauce over casserole, sprinkle with cheese and dust with paprika. Bake for 20 minutes at 375 degrees. serves 4. *Serve with rice.*

Gurd Tolley

SHRIMP AND CHEESE CASSEROLE

6 slices of bread
½ pound Old English cheese,
   sliced
1 pound shrimp, cooked and
   peeled

¼ cup butter, melted
3 eggs, beaten
½ teaspoon dry mustard
Salt
1 pint milk

Break bread and cheese into bite size pieces. Arrange bread, cheese and shrimp in several layers in greased casserole and pour melted butter over. Mix together remaining ingredients and pour over casserole. Cover and let stand a minimum of 3 hours, preferably overnight in the refrigerator. Bake at 350 degrees for 1 hour. Serves 4 to 6. *If doubling recipe, use 3 pounds of shrimp.*

Virginia Morrow

SHRIMP CREOLE

1 pound cleaned, cooked shrimp
4 tablespoons butter
Dash of vegetable oil
1 stalk celery, diced
1 small onion, diced
1 green pepepr, diced
½ pound sliced mushrooms

6 peeled, quartered fresh
  tomatoes
1 crumbled bay leaf
1 teaspoon salt
Dash of cayenne
Dash of black pepper

Saute shrimp in butter and vegetable oil. Remove from skillet and set aside. Add more oil to pan and add celery, onion, green pepper, and mushrooms. Saute until lightly browned. Add tomatoes, salt, cayenne, and pepper. Simmer 20 minutes or until thickened. Add shrimp. Reheat and serve over rice. Serves 4.

Barbara Brunton

SHRIMP CASSEROLE SURPRISE

1 cup macaroni, cooked, drained
  and cooled
2 hard boiled eggs, cooled, peeled
  and chopped
1 pound shrimp, cooked and
  peeled
1 cup tuna

⅓ cup chopped celery
⅓ cup chopped green pepper
1 teaspoon black pepper
1 teaspoon salt
¾ cup salad dressing
3 or 4 olives, chopped

In large bowl, mix first six ingredients. Let stand 10 minutes. Add next three ingredients. Arrange olives on top and refrigerate several hours before serving. Serves 8.

Claire Menge

SEAFOOD

SHRIMP JAMBALAYA

1 pound medium or large shrimp, peeled and deveined
½ cup light rum
½ cup water
1 large onion, coarsely chopped
¼ cup bacon fat

1 pound bulk sausage
3½ cups canned tomatoes
1 bay leaf
1½ teaspoons salt
¼ teaspoon thyme
1½ cups converted rice

Marinate shrimp in rum and water for 1 hour. Saute onion in bacon fat until lightly browned. Add sausage, broken into small pieces, and shrimp with rum and water. Simmer 2 to 3 minutes. Add remaining ingredients, cover and bring to a boil. Simmer 30 minutes. Serves 4 to 5. *Spinach salad is an excellent accompaniment.*

Craig Smith

SHRIMP IN HERB BUTTER SAUCE

1 pound shrimp, cooked and peeled
¼ cup butter
2 tablespoons lemon juice
1 teaspoon parsley flakes
1 teaspoon chives

½ teaspoon tarragon leaves
½ teaspoon dry mustard
¾ teaspoon Season All
⅛ teaspoon red pepper
¼ teaspoon onion powder

Melt butter, add remaining ingredients and saute 8 to 10 minutes. Serves 4.

Lois E. Taveredi

TUNA SCALLOP

½ cup stuffed green or ripe olives
5 slices white bread
1 can tuna, drained and flaked
1½ cups shredded Cheddar cheese
3 eggs

1½ cups milk
½ cup Chablis
¾ teaspoon seasoned salt
1 teaspoon Worcestershire sauce

Cut olives in generous wedges. Trim and discard crust from bread and cut into cubes. Arrange bread cubes, olives, tuna and cheese in 9x13-inch baking dish. Beat eggs with milk and Chablis. Mix in salt and Worcestershire sauce. Pour over ingredients in the casserole. Bake at 350 for about 60 minutes or until set in center. Serves 8.

Elizabeth von Schlichten

104

CHICKEN DIJON

2 whole chicken breasts, split,
  skinned and boned
1 cup milk
Flour
3 tablespoons vegetable oil
1 cup thinly sliced mushrooms
1 tablespoon butter

2 tablespoons dry white wine
1 (12-ounce) jar chicken gravy
⅔ cup half and half
1½ tablespoons Dijon-style
  mustard
Salt and pepper

Lightly flatten chicken breasts. Dip chicken in milk; coat generously with flour. Saute chicken in oil in skillet until golden brown, about four minutes per side. Remove; drain excess fat in skillet. Saute mushrooms in butter about 2 minutes. Adding remaining ingredients. Return chicken to skillet. Simmer, uncovered, 5 minutes. Serves 4.

Rod Henry
Mays Landing, New Jersey

CHICKEN PECAN QUICHE

1 pie shell (9-inch) baked and
  cooled
1 cup cooked chicken, finely
  chopped
1 cup grated Swiss cheese
¼ cup chopped onion

1 tablespoon flour
½ cup chopped pecans
2 eggs, beaten
1 cup milk
½ teaspoon brown mustard

Mix chicken, Swiss cheese, onion, flour and ¼ cup pecans. Sprinkle into cooled crust. Mix eggs, milk and mustard and pour over chicken mixture. Top with remaining ¼ cup pecans. Bake at 325 degrees for 50 minutes. Serves 6.

Dorothy Truman
New Castle, Delaware

CHICKEN-HAM ARTICHOKE CASSEROLE

2 cups chicken, cooked and diced
1 cup ham, cut in large chunks
1 can unmarinated artichokes,
   quartered
1 (10-ounce) can cream of chicken
   soup

½ cup good quality mayonnaise
½ teaspoon lemon juice
¼ teaspoon curry powder
2 sliced bread, toasted, buttered
   and cubed
1 cup Cheddar cheese, shredded

Layer chicken and ham in bottom of 1½ to 2-quart shallow casserole. Place artichokes on top. Combine soup, mayonnaise, lemon juice, curry powder, and pour over meats. Add cheese on top. Sprinkle bread crumbs on top. Bake uncovered at 350 degrees for 30 minutes. Serves 4 to 5.

QUICK CHICKEN CASSEROLE

1 can mushroom soup
1 can French style green beans,
   drained

1 small can boned chicken
1 can French onion rings
Slivered almonds

Combine soup, beans, chicken and ½ can onion rings; turn into baking dish. Cover with remianing onion rings; sprinkle with almonds. Bake in preheated 350 degree oven for 1 hour.

Denise Heckel

OVEN BAKED SESAME CHICKEN

6 to 8 boneless chicken breasts
3 cups buttermilk

l cup bread crumbs
½ cup sesame seeds

Marinate the chicken breasts in 2 cups of buttermilk overnight (turn 2 to 3 times. Place the bread crumbs and sesame seeds in a shallow dish. Dip the chicken in the bread crumb mixture and place in a baking pan or dish. Add the remaining buttermilk (1 cup). Bake at 350 degrees for 1 hour or until tender. Serves 6 to 8.

BAKED CHICKEN SALAD

1 can cream of chicken soup
1 can cream of mushroom soup
1 cup mayonnaise
2 tablespoons chopped onion
2 cups herb seasoned bread
  crumbs

2 cans water chestnuts, drained
  and sliced
4½ cups cubed cooked chicken
½ cup grated Cheddar cheese

Combine soups and mayonnaise. Toss with remaining ingredients, except cheese. Bake in 2-quart casserole or shallow 12x8x2-inch dish at 350 degrees for 40 to 45 minutes. Top with cheese the last 10 minutes. Serves 6.

Anne Postles
Milford, Delaware

BARBECUED CHICKEN LEA MING

3 boned, skinned chicken breasts
½ soy sauce
5 tablespoons brown sugar
½ clove garlic, minced

¼ teaspoon ground ginger
1 tablespoon vegetable oil
1 teaspoon curry powder
Bamboo skewers

Cut chicken breasts in ¾ inch strips. Mix other ingredients and marinate chicken strips in it for 20 to 30 minutes. Soak bamboo skewers in water. Thread chicken on the skewers. Broil quickly over hot charcoal for 15 minutes, turning every 5 minutes. Serves 6. *Lea Ming is a family recipe.*

Sue Leaming

CASHEW CHICKEN

2 pounds boneless chicken
½ teaspoon salt
1½ cups flour

½ cup milk
2 eggs, beaten
Peanut oil

Mix salt and flour. Cut chicken in small pieces and flour well. Let stand in flour mixture for 15 minutes. Mix milk and eggs. Remove chicken from flour mixture and add to egg mixture. Let stand for 10 minutes. Roll again in flour mixture and deep fry in peanut oil. Keep warm in oven.

Sauce
2 cans chicken broth
2 to 4 tablespoons cornstarch
2 to 4 tablespoons water

3 tablespoons soy sauce
Green onions, chopped
Cashew nuts

Combine first 4 ingredients and cook over medium heat until thick. Pour over fried chicken on platter and top with chopped green onions and cashew nuts. Serve over wild rice. Serves 4. *Chicken can be prepared for frying ahead of time.*

Linda Amos

CHICKEN AND STUFFING STRATA

½ package (8-ounces) herb
   stuffing mix
1½ cups chopped cooked chicken
¼ cup minced celery
3 eggs

2½ cups milk
1 teaspoon salt
2 ounces shredded Swiss cheese
   (½ cup)

Sprinkle half of the stuffing mix in a buttered 12x8x2-inch pan. Sprinkle chicken, celery and onion over stuffing. Top with remaining stuffing mix. Beat eggs, milk and salt together. Pour over stuffing and sprinkle with cheese. Cover and refrigerate one hour or overnight. Bake at 375 degrees for 45 minutes, or until puffed and golden. Let stand 10 minutes before serving. Serves 4.

Julie Merson

CHICKEN BREASTS MARSALA

4 boned chicken breasts
2 beaten eggs
Bread crumbs for breading
Butter for frying
½ pound fresh mushrooms

4 tablespoons butter
1¼ cup flour
1 chicken bouillon cube in 1 cup
    water
½ cup Marsala wine

Dip chicken in eggs and bread crumbs. Cook in butter in frying pan until done. Remove chicken from pan and keep warm. Blend 4 tablespoons butter and flour in cast iron frying pan. Add bouillon to pan and blend. Add Marsala wine and cook until thickened. Add mushrooms that have been sauteed in butter. Simmer. Pour over cooked chicken and serve immediately. Serves 4.

Ruth Rutherford

CHICKEN BREASTS VERONIQUE

8 tablespoons butter
2 to 3 whole boneless, skinless
    chicken breasts, split
8 ounces small mushrooms,
    quartered
¼ pound lean ham, diced
3 tablespoons all-purpose flour

1 cup dry white wine
2 cups half-and-half, scalded
Salt
Freshly ground pepper
½ pound seedless green grapes,
    halved

Preheat oven to 350 degrees. Grease a 2-quart casserole. In a skillet melt half the butter over moderate heat. Add chicken and saute until browned. Put chicken in casserole. Mix in ham and mushrooms. Add remaining butter to the skillet and stir in flour. Cook for several minutes and add wine and half-and-half. Cook, constantly stirring until mixture thickens. Season with salt and pepper. Pour the white sauce over chicken, ham and mushrooms. Bake for 30 minutes. Add grapes and bake 10 minutes more. Serves 4 to 6. *A great combination of tastes.*

Anne Postles
Milford, Delaware

CHICKEN FIESTA

2 tablespoons butter
1½ tablespoons flour
1⅓ cups light cream
½ teaspoon salt
¼ teaspoon paprika
⅛ teaspoon pepper

¾ cup shredded carrots
⅓ cup diced green pepper
2½ cups cooked diced chicken
¾ cup sliced mushrooms (optional)
Patty shells

In a medium saucepan, heat butter until melted. Stir in flour and cook 1 minute, stirring constantly. Remove from heat and stir in cream, beating until smooth. Cook 5 minutes over moderate heat, stirring constantly. Stir in the remaining ingredients (except patty shells) and cook 8 to 10 minutes until thoroughly heated through. Spoon into baked warm patty shells. Serves 6. *This can be made ahead and frozen.*

Florence L. D. Heal

CHICKEN DIVINE

4 whole chicken breasts (6 cups)
1½ cups finely chopped celery
1 can sliced water chestnuts

1 cup mayonnaise
Salt and pepper
Cornbread stuffing

Boil chicken, skin and bone, but do not dice. Mix all ingredients and place in greased casserole. Cover with cornbread stuffing that has been prepared with butter and white wine and chicken broth and lightly tossed. Bake at 350 degrees for 30 minutes until bubbly crisp. Serves 6. *Cover with foil to freeze; can be made weeks ahead.*

Anita M. Laird

CHICKEN CACCIATORE
Must be prepared l day in advance

6 tablespoons olive oil
2½ to 3 pounds fryer chicken, cut up
¾ cup green pepper, chopped
l cup onions, minced
4 garlic cloves, minced
l large can Italian tomatoes
l (8-ounce) can tomato sauce

½ cup red wine
3 teaspoons salt
½ teaspoon pepper
2 bay leaves
½ teaspoon oregano
½ teaspoon thyme
Dash cayenne pepper
l pound noodles, cooked

Brown chicken in olive oil. Remove chicken and put aside. Brown onions, pepper and garlic in oil. Add tomatoes, tomato sauce, wine and spices. Simmer at least 20 minutes or more. Spoon sauce over chicken and let marinate 24 hours. Reheat at 350 degrees for l hour and serve over cooked noodles. Serves 4 to 5.

Rona Craig

CHICKEN DIVAN

8 chicken breasts, halved
2 boxes frozen broccoli spears
l pound fresh mushrooms, sliced
l can cream of mushroom soup
l can cream of chicken soup
l cup mayonnaise
Splash of sherry

l (l0-ounce) stick sharp Cheddar cheese, grated
l cup butter, divided
3 cups bread crumbs
l bay leaf
Salt to taste
l teaspoon lemon juice

Boil chicken in large pot of water with salt and bay leaf for approximately 45 minutes. When finished, remove chicken from bone and cut into bite-size pieces. Saute mushrooms in half of butter until cooked. Salt to taste. Drain. Cook frozen broccoli until al dente. Drain. Cut into bite-size pieces. Make sauce from soup and mayonnaise. Add sherry to taste. Mix bread crumbs with rest of butter, melted. In large baking dish, place layers as follows: chicken, broccoli, chicken, broccoli, mushrooms, sauce, Cheddar cheese and bread crumbs. Bake at 350 degrees for 45 minutes. Serves 6 to 8. *Can be made ahead.*

B. Michael Zuckerman

CHICKEN CASSEROLE

1½ cups cooked, diced chicken
½ pound fresh sauteed
  mushrooms
2 ounces cooked spaghetti
¼ cup milk

¼ cup sour cream
1 can cream of chicken soup
4 ounces shredded Cheddar
  cheese
Slivered almonds (optional)

Mix all ingredients except cheese. Place in casserole. Cover with cheese. Top with almonds if desired. Bake, uncovered, at 375 degrees for 30 minutes. Serves 4. *This easy recipe can be made ahead and frozen.*

Mary Trexler

CHICKEN PESTO

2 pounds skinless, boneless
  chicken breasts

2 cups chicken broth
Salt and pepper to taste

In a covered pan, simmer chicken in broth for 20 to 25 minutes. Cool in broth, then drain and cut into 1½-inch chunks. Set aside.

Pesto Sauce
2 cups loosely packed fresh basil
2 garlic cloves
⅓ cup walnuts or pine nuts

¼ cup Parmesan cheese
6 tablespoons olive oil
2 cups cooked peas

Mix first 4 ingredients in blender or processor and use several off/on turns until blended. Slowly add oil to make a smooth paste. Add sauce to coat chicken. Gently add peas. Serves 4. *Can be a main dish or served as a salad on lettuce.*

Betty Deal
Medford, New Jersey

MAINSTAY CHICKEN PIE

8 cups cooked, diced chicken
½ cup milk
½ cup sour cream

2 cans cream of chicken soup,
  undiluted

Heat all ingredients and pour into 13x9-inch pan or 2-quart casserole.

Topping
½ teaspoon salt
1 beaten egg
¾ cup milk

½ cup cornmeal
1 cup buttermilk pancake mix
2 cups shredded Cheddar cheese

Combine all except cheese. Blend and then fold in cheese. Spoon on top of hot chicken mixture. Bake, uncovered, at 375 degrees for 20 to 30 minutes. Serves 8. *An award winning recipe.*

Mainstay Inn

CURRY CHICKEN WITH BROCCOLI

6 pieces of chicken breast
2 (10-ounce) packages chopped
  broccoli
2 (10-ounce) cans cream of
  mushroom soup

¾ cup mayonnaise
½ cup melted butter
2 cups herb bread crumbs
2 tablespoons lemon juice
½ teaspoon curry powder

Cook and bone chicken. Arrange chicken in shallow baking dish. Cook and drain broccoli. Arrange on chicken. In another bowl, mix soup, mayonnaise, lemon juice and curry powder. Pour over chicken and broccoli. Mix the crumbs and butter. Sprinkle on top. Bake at 350 degrees for 30 minutes. Serves 6. *Easy and can be made ahead and frozen.*

Sue Leaming

CHOICE CHICKEN BAKE

4 chicken breasts
l package dried beef
l can mushroom soup

½ soup can of sour cream
4 slices bacon

Split, bone and skin chicken breasts. Pull dried beef apart in small pieces. Spread beef in the bottom of l4xl0-inch casserole. Place chicken breasts on top of beef. Mix mushroom soup and sour cream. Pour over chicken. Place ½ strip of bacon on each ½ of chicken. Bake at 300 degrees for 2 hours. Serves 6.

Claire Sandbach
Wilmington, Delaware

THREE "C" CASSEROLE

l (3-ounce) can chow mein noodles
l can whole cashews
l½ to 2 cups cooked chicken
l (l0-ounce) can cream of

mushroom soup
½ cup chicken stock or milk
2 tablespoons soy sauce

Combine half chow mein noodles and nuts with all other ingredients in a shallow, greased casserole. Mix well. Add more liquid if needed. Top with remaining noodles and nuts. Bake 350 degrees for 30 minutes. Serves 6.

Ada Tuttle

SWEET AND SOUR CHICKEN

1 (8-ounce) bottle Russian
  dressing
1 envelope dry onion soup mix
1 (8-ounce) jar of apricot or peach
preserves

6 to 8 chicken pieces
3 cups rice, cooked according to
  directions

Combine first 3 ingredients. Mix well. Set aside. Lightly grease 13x9-inch baking dish. Lay chicken pieces in a single layer. Pour sauce over all. Bake, uncovered, at 350 degrees for 60 minutes. Serve over rice. Serves 5 to 6.

RED CHICKEN JAMBALAYA

2 pounds chicken pieces
1 pound smoked sausage
½ pound smoked ham
¼ cup corn oil
4 cups chopped onions
2 cups chopped celery
2 cups chopped green pepper
2 tablespoons chopped garlic
5 cups chicken stock
1 cup tomato sauce
½ teaspoon oregano

1 teaspoon thyme
3 teaspoons salt
¼ teaspoon cayenne pepper
¼ teaspoon white pepper
¼ teaspoon black pepper
2 bay leaves
½ cup chopped parsley
1 cup chopped scallions
1 cup chopped tomatoes
3 to 4 cups long grain rice

In a thick bottom pot, season and brown chicken over medium high heat in half the oil. Add the ham and sausage. Saute with the chicken. Remove all three from pot. In same pot, add rest oil, saute onions, celery, green pepper and garlic, just until tender. Return chicken, ham, sausage to pot. Add stock and bring to boil. Add salt, peppers, herbs, seasoning, and tomato sauce. Add rice and return to boil. Cover. Reduce to simmer. Cook for 30 minutes total. After 10 minutes quickly remove rice from sides of pot. Stir once. At end of 30 minutes, add scallions, parsley, and fresh chopped tomatoes. Toss and serve at once. Serves 4 to 6.

410 Bank Street Restaurant

RANGER CHICKEN

1 clove garlic (crushed)
½ cup chopped onion
1 tablespoon oil
¾ cup grated carrots
¾ pound bulk sausage

½ cup red wine
6 boned chicken breasts
   (flattened)
Vegetable juice cocktail

Saute garlic and onion in oil. Add carrots, sausage, and red wine. Cook until sausage is done. Drain off juices and fat from sausage mix. Overlap two flattened breasts and line one edge with ⅓ saute mix. Roll like jelly roll. Repeat until all ingredients are used. Place rolls side by side in a 9x9-inch baking dish. Cover with vegetable juice. Bake at 350 degrees for 35 minutes. Slice on the diagonal and serve with gravy from pan. Serves 6.

J. D. Roth

QUICKIE CHICKIE

5 pounds chicken parts
¼ cup melted butter
Garlic powder to taste
3 (10¾-ounce) cans cream of
   mushroom soup
½ cup sweet vermouth

½ cup chopped parsley
½ teaspoon poultry seasoning
Optional: fresh or canned
   mushrooms
Paprika

In two 12x8-inch dishes arrange chicken in single layer skin-side up. Brush with butter to which garlic has been added. Bake at 400 degrees for 45 minutes. Baste once with pan drippings. Sprinkle with mushrooms. Combine soup, vermouth, parsley, and poultry seasoning. Spoon over chicken and mushrooms and sprinkle with paprika. Bake 15 minutes more or until slightly browned. Serves 10. *Easy for entertaining and can be made ahead.*

Dorothy H. Mikus
Cranford, New Jersey

OLD FASHIONED CHICKEN POT PIE

1 large stewing chicken, cut up
2½ cups flour
½ cup shortening
½ teaspoon salt

Cover chicken with water and stew. Rub flour, shortening and salt together to consistency of pie dough. Add just enough water (about 4 tablespoons) to make the dough easy to handle. Roll dough out on a floured surface about ¼-inch thick. Cut dough in squares about 2x2-inches. After stewing chicken, remove all pieces from broth and place them in a baking pan. Sprinkle chicken with salt, pepper and parsley. Put all the dough squares in the broth and simmer for 45 minutes to 1 hour, 10 minutes before dumplings are done, broast chicken pieces under the broiler until brown. Serves 4.

Dorothy Garrabrant
North Wildwood, New Jersey

MOO GOO GAI PIEN

2 tablespoons cornstarch, divided
½ teaspoon salt
2 whole boneless chicken breast, cut in 1-inch cubes
1 tablespoon soy sauce
1 tablespoon sherry
3 tablespoons vegetable oil
2 green onions, sliced
½ pound fresh mushrooms, sliced
½ teaspoon garlic powder
¼ teaspoon ground ginger
1 (10¾-ounce) can cream of chicken soup
1 (7-ounce) package frozen peas pods, thawed
1 (7-ounce) can water chestnuts, drained and sliced
3 to 4 cups cooked rice

Combine 1 tablespoon cornstarch and salt in a bowl. Add chicken cubes and coat well. Combine soy sauce, sherry, and remaining cornstarch in a separate bowl, blending well. Set aside. Heat oil in a wok or electric skillet to 375 degrees. Add chicken and cook, stirring constantly, for 2 to 3 minutes. Remove chicken and add onion and mushrooms to the pan. Add garlic powder and ginger. Cook, stirring constantly, for 1 minute. Stir in chicken soup. Add soy sauce mix slowly, stirring until thick. Add pea pods, water chestnuts, and chicken. Cook until heated. Serve over rice. Serves 4. *An oriental classic made easy!*

Rona Craig

JAKE'S CHICKEN

2 whole boned chicken breasts
Flour for dredging
½ cup butter
½ cup white wine

2 tablespoons chives
1 cup sliced mushrooms, canned
½ pint sour cream

Cut chicken into "finger." Dredge in flour. Brown in butter for several minutes until cooked (about 4 minutes). Sprinkle chives and mushrooms over chicken and stir. Add sour cream and stir again until smooth. Total cooking time is 10 minutes. Serves 4. *Our son Jake's very favorite.*

Helen Fox

CRUNCHY DRUMSTICKS

1 cup orange juice
1 tablespoon oil
1 tablespoon salt
¼ teaspoon pepper

3 pounds chicken drumsticks
¼ cup margarine
1¼ cups uncooked oats

Early in the day mix orange juice, salt and pepper in a 13x9-inch dish. Add chicken and coat with juice. Cover and refrigerate 4 hours, turning often. About 1 hour before serving, preheat oven to 400 degrees. Line a jelly roll pan with foil. Add margarine and melt in oven. Meanwhile, on waxed paper coat chicken in oats. Arrange chicken in one layer in pan, coating with margarine. Bake 40 to 50 minutes until chicken is tender, turning once. Serve hot or cold. Serves 8.

Jean Anne Christie
Wayne, New Jersey

CRISPY PEPPERY CHICKEN

1 (3-pound) chicken, cut in eighths
1 cup milk
1 cup flour, divided
½ cup cornmeal
1½ teaspoons salt

¾ to 1¼ teaspoons ground black
  pepper
2 eggs, beaten
1 quart safflower oil

Place chicken in a medium bowl. Pour milk over chicken. Cover and refrigerate for 1 hour. In a bowl or plastic bag, combine ½ cup of the flour, cornmeal salt and pepper. Place remaining ½ cup flour in another bowl or bag. Place eggs in a separate bowl. Drain chicken. Coat a few pieces of chicken at a time with flour, then eggs, and finally with cornmeal mixture. Heat oil in a large saucepan to 350 degrees. Fry a few pieces of chicken at a time until cooked through and golden, 10 to 15 minutes. Drain on paper towels. Serves 4. *Moist chicken with lots of crunch!*

Mena Potts
Wintersville, Ohio

CHICKEN TAMALE

6 whole chicken breasts
1 (26-ounce) can tamales, cut up
1 (6-ounce) can ripe pitted olives,
  cut in half
1 (10-ounce) can cream of chicken
  soup
1 (28-ounce) can tomatoes,
  including juice

1 pint sour cream
2 tablespoons onions
1 teaspoon chopped garlic
Salt and pepper to taste
½ cup grated cheese

Cook and dice chicken. Combine all other ingredients with chicken. Pour into casserole and cover with grated cheese. Bake at 350 degrees for 40 minutes. Let sit 10 minutes before serving. Serves 10 to 12.

Katie Gregg

CHICKEN IN SHERRY SAUCE

6 chicken breasts, boned, skinned
 and cut in half
Flour
Salt and pepper
½ pound mushrooms, sauteed

1 can cream of mushroom soup
1 can cream of chicken soup
¾ cup sherry
Chicken drippings

Roll chicken in seasoned flour, brown in butter and place in casserole. Add mushrooms. Combine soups, sherry and chicken drippings. Pour over chicken and bake in covered casserole at 350 degrees for 1¼ hours. Serve over rice. Serves 10 to 12.

Alberta Craig

CHICKEN SALTIMBOCCA

3 large chicken breasts boned and
 skinned
6 thin slices boiled ham
6 slices Swiss cheese
1 medium tomato, peeled, chopped

⅓ cup bread crumbs
2 tablespoons Parmesan cheese,
 grated
2 tablespoons parsley
¼ cup butter, melted

Cut each chicken breast in half lengthwise. Pound each piece of chicken to ⅛ inch thickness. Place ham slice and cheese slice on each cutlet. Top with tomato. Fold in sides, and roll up jelly roll fashion. Combine crumbs, cheese and parsley. Dip chicken in butter, then roll in crumbs. Bake in shallow baking pan at 350 degrees for 40 to 45 minutes. Serves 6. *Very easy and can be frozen.*

Lori Schue

CHICKEN IN RED WINE VINEGAR

4 boned, skinned chicken breasts
½ cup dried minced onions

Red wine vinegar, enough to
 cover half of the breast (½ to 1
 cup)

Place chicken in glass baking dish. Sprinkle with dried onion. Pour vinegar over chicken. Bake at 350 degrees 30 to 45 minutes. Serves 4. *This recipe can be expanded very easily. Broccoli and carrot stir fry is great accompaniment.*

Christy Igoe
Seaville, New Jersey

120

CHICKEN IN RASPBERRY CREAM

8 chicken breasts, skinned, boned
  and floured
4 tablespoons butter
2 tablespoons oil

¾ cup raspberry vinegar
1½ cups chicken stock
1½ cups heavy whipping cream

Saute chicken in butter and oil. Remove from pan and keep warm. Add raspberry vinegar to pan and bring to a boil. Add chicken stock and chicken. Simmer for 10 to 12 minutes. Remove chicken and keep warm. Boil liquid until it becomes thick. Add whipping cream and allow to thicken again over medium heat. Serve sauce over chicken. Serves 8.

Washington Inn

CHICKEN KIEV

½ cup butter
½ tablespoon chopped parsley
½ tablespoon chopped chives
1 tablespoon lemon juice
6 chicken breasts, boned

Salt and freshly ground pepper
2 cups fine dry bread crumbs
3 eggs lightly beaten
3 tablespoons water
Oil for deep frying

Blend butter, parsley, chives and lemon juice in a small bowl. Refrigerate. Place chicken breasts between two pieces of waxed paper. Pound well to flatten. Remove paper. Sprinkle with salt and pepper. Divide seasoned butter into 6 portions. Place portion of butter in center of each breast. Fold short ends of breast into center, then fold in sides to make a "package." Secure with wooden toothpicks. Add water to eggs and mix. Coat each rolled breast with bread crumbs. Dip into egg mixture, then crumbs again, coating well. Chill 1 hour. Heat oil in deep fryer to 365 degrees. Carefully lower breasts into hot oil. Fry 8 minutes or until golden brown. Drain on paper towel. Serves 6.

Elizabeth von Schlichten

SWEET SPICY CHICKEN BREASTS

5 chicken breasts with wings
½ cup Worcestershire sauce

½ cup lemon juice
¼ cup sugar

Place chicken breasts in a baking dish, wing side up. Combine remaining ingredients in a saucepan and heat through. Pour over chicken and cover tightly. Bake at 350 degrees for 1 hour for until tender. Baste occasionally. Serves 3 to 5. *I like to serve this dish with salt roasted new potatoes and corn on the cob.*

Christy Igoe
Seaville, New Jersey

ONE PAN PAELLA

16 Little Neck clams
20 medium shrimp
1 pound sweet sausage
1 pound chicken, boned, skinned,
  cut in strips
1 large Spanish onion
1½ cups chicken broth
1 cup water
1 cup converted rice

1 clove garlic chopped
Pinch crushed red pepper
1 large green bell pepper
1 large red bell pepper
1 tablespoon basil
Salt and pepper
½ teaspoon saffron threads
8 fresh peeled tomatoes

Wash clams and cover with lightly salted water for 15 minutes. Cut sausage into ½ inch pieces and fry in large skillet until brown and done, remove from pan and retain fat in pan. Add chicken and cook until done, remove from pan. Add 1 cup chicken broth to deglaze pan. Add chopped garlic, onions, pepper and shrimp. Cook until tender. Add crushed fresh tomatoes, basil and saffron. Return chicken and sausage to pan. Stir to mix. Salt and pepper to taste. Add 1 cup chicken broth and 1 cup water, stir in rice, add crushed red pepper and whole clams. Stir to mix ingredients. Cover and simmer until liquid is absorbed. Serve at once. *Quick and easy pan method of a classic dish. Great for you men who want to surprise your wife once in a while.*

Scott Glenn, Chef/Atlas Motor Inn

COLD CHICKEN CURRY

2 chickens, cooked and cooled
2 small onions, minced
4 ounces oil
4 tablespoons curry powder
8 ounces red wine
6 ounces water
2 teaspoons tomato puree

Juice from a lemon
2 to 3 lemon slices
½ teaspoon sugar
Salt and pepper to taste
Bay leaf
1 cup plain yogurt or mayonnaise

Debone and cut chicken into cubes. Refrigerate. Saute onions in oil but do not brown. Add curry powder, wine, water and tomato puree. Squeeze lemon juice into mixture. Add lemon slices, sugar, salt, pepper, and bay leaf. Cook this mixture for about 10 minutes. Strain the essence and refrigerate. When ready to serve, add yogurt or mayonnaise to chicken and pour essence into mixture. Toss and serve on lettuce. Serves 10 to 12.

Mary Kosak

HOLIDAY CORNISH HEN

4 Cornish hens (about 1½ pounds
  each)
4 teaspoons fresh lemon
½ teaspoon salt

⅛ teaspoon pepper
¼ cup butter or margarine
  (melted)
1 cup chopped parsley

Stuffing
1 cup cooked rice
¼ cup raisins
½ pound cooked, crumbled Italian
  sausage

1 beaten egg
⅓ cup grated Parmesan cheese
2 cups water

Sprinkle the inside and outside of rinsed hens with the lemon juice, salt and pepper. Reserve the butter and chopped parsley to baste the hen every 15 minutes while cooking. Combine the stuffing ingredients in a large bowl. Toss lightly to mix. Spoon about ½ cup into each cavity. Extra stuffing can be place in buttered custard cups. Roast hens at 375 degrees for 1 to 1½ hours. Arrange on large platter, garnish with grapes or cranberries. Serve 4. *A nice alternative to turkey.*

Charlotte Todd

TURKEY PICCATA

1 pound turkey cutlets
2 tablespoons butter
½ cup lemon juice
Salt and pepper to taste

1 cup sauteed mushrooms
½ cup sherry or marsala wine
2 tablespoons chopped parsley

Flatten cutlets and pat dry. Melt butter in skillet. Saute mushrooms and set aside. Saute cutlets 2 to 3 minutes on each side. Remove. Add lemon juice, salt and pepper, and sherry to skillet and bring to boil, scraping all browned particles from bottom of pan. Pour over cutlets and mushrooms. Sprinkle with parsley and serve. Serves 4. *So easy and quite elegant!*

Jean T. Timmons

EASY TURKEY TETRAZZINI

1 cup turkey broth
1 can cream of chicken soup
1 can cream of mushroom soup
2 cups grated processed cheese
6 cups cooked spaghetti

4 cups diced cooked turkey
½ cup sliced mushrooms
½ cup grated Parmesan cheese
Paprika to taste

Mix broth and soups and stir in the processed cheese. Mix with the spaghetti, turkey and mushrooms. Turn into one 12x8-inch shallow baking dish. Sprinkle with Parmesan cheese and paprika. Bake at 350 degrees for about ½ hour or until brown and bubbly. Serves 8 to 10.

STEAK ROMANO

2 bell peppers, sliced
2 medium onions, sliced
2 cloves garlic
4 steak filets

¼ cup brandy for flambe
¼ cup red wine
Salt and pepper to taste
4 slices mozzarella cheese

Saute peppers, onions and garlic in butter. Braise filets, add brandy and flambe in same pan. Add sauteed ingredients and red wine, cover. Cook 4 minutes for rare, 6 minutes for medium, 8 minutes for well done. Add cheese slices on each filet, cover until melted. Serve 4. *Excellent served with wild rice and a Caesar salad*

Josie Davies, Keltie News

CAREFREE STEW

2 pounds stewing beef cubes
6 carrots, cut in strips
1 green pepper, cut in strips
3 potatoes, cut in strips
½ turnip, cut in strips
1 diced onion

5 stalks celery, diced
2½ cups stewed tomatoes
1 teaspoon salt
1 tablespoon sugar
3 tablespoons instant tapioca

Put all ingredients in covered baking dish. Bake at 300 degrees for 4 hours, stirring occasionally. Serves 12.

Laura Wilkinson
Radnor, Pennsylvania

CHINESE CASSEROLE

1 pound chopped meat, browned
1 cup chopped celery
2 medium chopped onion
1 can cream of celery or
   mushroom soup

1½ cups water
1 can sliced water chestnuts
⅛ cup soy sauce
½ teaspoon pepper

After browning meat, combine all ingredients. Put in a casserole, cover and bake at 350 degrees for 30 to 45 minutes. Serve with Chinese noodles. Serves 4. *This is very easy and can be made ahead and frozen.*

LaVerne Stickles
Florham Park, New Jersey

BEEF ROLL-UPS

2 cups seasoned stuffing mix
⅔ cup hot water
1 to 2 pieces cubed beef, enough
   for 4 (6x6-inch) pieces

2 tablespoons oil
Brown gravy (mix, canned, or
   homemade)

Combine stuffing mix with water. Spread each cubed steak with stuffing mixture. Roll and fasten with wooden picks. Brown beef rolls in oil in skillet. Drain. Place rolls in a shallow baking dish with favorite brown gravy and bake at 325 degrees for 20 minutes. Serves 4.

Lori Schue

WINDSOR BAKED STEAK

3 tablespoons oil, divided
1 medium onion, sliced
2 cloves garlic, minced or sliced
1 green pepper, sliced into halved
   strips
½ pound mushrooms, sliced
2 large tomatoes, cut into wedges

¼ cup sherry or white wine
½ teaspoon salt (optional)
¼ teaspoon freshly ground black
   pepper
1 (½-inch) thick sirloin, (1½ pound
   serves 3)
3 slices crisp bacon

Preheat oven to 500 degrees and set to bake. Place 2 tablespoon olive oil in saucepan over medium heat, saute onion, garlic, green pepper, and mushrooms until soft. Add tomatoes, wine, salt, pepper and simmer over low heat for 10 minutes. Keep warm. Place 1 tablespoon olive oil in shallow baking dish, and spread to cover bottom. Add steak and place in oven. Turn steak at 5 minutes intervals and season with salt and pepper to taste at last turning. Allow 20 minutes for rare, 30 for medium, and 30 to 35 for well. When done to taste, remove the steak to a hot platter and arrange cooked vegetables around it. Top with bacon slices and garnish with fresh parsley. Serve immediately with steak knives all-round, and your favorite starch (bread, rice, noodles, or potatoes). Serves 3 to 4. *This is a personal recipe of the Duchess of Windsor (with minimal modifications by the Bailey family). You remember the Duchess: Wallis (Wally) Warfield Simpson, a Cape May deb. Her lover, Edward VIII, abdicated his succession as King of England to marry her - a scandal that still rocks proper Britains. If "the way to a man's heart" is via the stomach, perhaps this recipe may be the kind of stuff for which kings give up thrones. Anyway, the Duchess published her favorite recipes in a series of newspaper articles in the late fifties. My mother clipped this one from the Fort Lauderdale News, page 4-D, Thursday, October 30, 1958. It has also become a favorite around our Windsor Castle.*

John Bailey, The Baileywicke

PEPPER STEAK

2 tablespoons cornstarch
2 tablespoons soy sauce
½ teaspoon salt
1 pound round steak, cut in thin
  strips
4 tablespoons oil, divided

1 pound green peppers, cut in
  1½-inch pieces
½ teaspoon garlic powder
1 (10¾-ounce) can beef consomme
1 tomato cut in 8 wedges
1 cup mushrooms, sauteed

Combine cornstarch, soy sauce and salt with a little water and marinate beef. Heat 2 tablespoons oil in skillet. Add peppers, saute over high heat for 1 minute. Remove peppers and add remaining oil and garlic. Over high heat, saute seasoned beef rapidly, turning constantly for 2 minutes. Return peppers, pour in beef consomme and remaining marinade. Bring to a fast boil. At this point, add the tomatoes. Cook until juices thicken, but do not overcook. Add mushrooms and simmer until thoroughly warmed. Serve with rice. Serves 4.

Karen Hallberg
Wilmington, Delaware

PORCUPINE MEAT BALLS

1 pound ground chuck beef
½ cup uncooked rice
Salt
Pepper
1 chopped onion

1 can tomato soup
1 cup hot water
Dash garlic powder
Pinch of oregano

Combine meat, rice, salt, pepper, and onion. Shape into 12 balls. In heavy saucepan, combine soup, water, garlic powder and oregano. Bring to boil. Drop meatballs into soup mixture. Reduce heat and simmer for approximately 1½ hours or until rice is tender. Serves 3 to 4. *An easy and good meal!*

Barbara Brunton

REUBEN MEATLOAF

1 egg, beaten
1 cup soft rye bread crumbs
½ cup chopped onion
¼ cup sweet pickle relish
¼ cup Russian salad dressing
1 tablespoon Worcestershire sauce

Salt and pepper to taste
1½ pounds lean ground beef or
  pork
1 (8-ounce) can sauerkraut,
  drained and chopped
1 cup shredded Swiss Cheese

Combine egg, bread crumbs, onion, relish, salad dressing, Worcestershire sauce, salt and pepper. Add ground meat and mix well on waxed paper. Pat mixture into a 12x8-inch rectangle, top with sauerkraut and ¾ cup of the cheese. Roll up meat in a jelly roll style, beginning with short side. Press ends to seal. Place roll, seam side down, in a 13x9x2-inch baking pan. Bake at 350 degrees for 50 minutes. Sprinkle remaining cheese on top. Bake 3 minutes more. Serves 8.

Trudy Jarret
Jax Beach, Florida

BEEF IN SHERRY

1½ pounds top round steak
1 garlic bud, used whole
1 teaspoon salt
¼ teaspoon flavor enhancer
1 small package cream cheese

1 small can button mushrooms
4 ounces cream sherry
1 cup rice prepared according to
  directions

Cut steak into bite-size pieces and brown in butter. Cover scantily with water. Add garlic bud, salt, flavor enhancer and sherry. Cook until beef is tender, approximately 1 hour. Soften cream cheese with some gravy, beating until smooth. Add more gravy to make thinner and add to meat mixture. Add mushrooms and thicken gravy to consistency of heavy cream. Simmer. Serve with rice. Serves 4.

Grace Hathaway

DUDE RANCH MEATBALL BAKE

1 (16-ounce) can tomatoes, chopped
1 (15¾-ounce) can barbecued beans
1 egg, beaten
¾ cup instant mashed potato
　flakes
½ envelope dry onion soup mix
2 tablespoons catsup
2 teaspoons Worcestershire sauce
1 pound lean ground beef
½ cup flour
1½ teaspoons baking powder
¼ teaspoon chili powder
¼ cup milk
2 tablespoons oil

Combine undrained tomatoes and beans. Turn into 16x6x2-inch baking dish. Combine egg, potato flakes, soup mix, catsup, Worcestershire sauce and ground beef. Mix well and shape into 18 to 20 meatballs. Arrange meatballs on beans. Bake, covered, at 375 degrees for 35 minutes. Meanwhile stir together flour, baking powder and chili powder. Add milk and oil and mix into a batter. Drop batter by spoonfuls between meatballs. Return to oven and bake 20 minutes more.

Trudy Jarret
Jax Beach, Florida

HACHE

½ cup butter
1 pound stewing beef, cubed
½ pound onions, sliced
5 cloves
6 bay leaves
1 cup water

Melt butter in large pot, add meat and brown. Stir in onions, cloves and bay leaves and water and simmer until meat is tender, about 1½ to 2 hours. (You might have to add more water due to evaporation). Serves 4 to 6.

Captain Mey's Inn, Inn Keepers Carin Fedderman, Milly Lacanfora

MARINATED TENDERLOIN

1½ pounds beef tenderloin
¼ cup red wine
1 tablespoon brandy or sherry
3 tablespoons olive oil
1 to 2 sliced garlic cloves
Dash of salt
1 bay leaf crushed

Put beef in a plastic bag. Combine all other ingredients and pour over beef. Close bag and marinate 24 hours in refrigerator turning occasionally. Roast beef at 450 degrees for 30 to 45 minutes. Serves 6.

CHRISTY'S CHILI

1 to 2 pounds ground beef	1 large can kidney beans
Large onion	2 large cans tomato sauce
4 to 6 cans tomato soup	Oregano and chili powder to taste
1 large can sliced mushrooms	

Brown ground beef and onion. Add all other ingredients and let simmer 1 to 3 hours, uncovered, stirring frequently. Add as much oregano and chili powder to taste, but at least 2 tablespoons oregano and 1 tablespoon chili powder. Serves 4 to 8. *This easy recipe can be made ahead and freezes well. Great over spaghetti or macaroni.*

Christy Igoe
Seaville, New Jersey

JIM'S FAVORITE CHILI

1½ pounds ground chuck	½ to 1 cup Rotelle chili peppers
1 cup chopped onion	¼ teaspoon cinnamon
2 cloves minced garlic	Dash ground cloves
1 stalk celery, chopped	8 to 10 ounces V-8 juice
1 green pepper, chopped	1 handful brown rice
Chili powder to taste	2 (16-ounce) cans red kidney beans

Brown ground beef and drain. Saute onion, garlic, celery, and green pepper. Add chili pepper (to taste), spices, juice, ground beef, and rice. Simmer 1 hour. Add beans. Simmer 30 minutes. Serve with shredded Cheddar cheese on top. Serves 6 to 8.

Patricia Rafftesaeth
Lansdale, Pennsylvania

SUKIYAKI

2 tablespoons sugar
1 teaspoon MSG
Beef Suet
1 pound beef tenderloin, sliced paper thin across grain
1 large or 2 small chicken breasts, sliced paper thin across grain
4 loin pork chops, sliced paper thin across grain
2 cups green onions, cut bias in 2-inch lengths

½ cup thin sliced mushrooms
½ cup soy sauce
½ cup beef stock or broth
1 package fresh spinach (can substitute thin sliced cabbage)
1 cup celery, cut bias in 2-inch lengths
1 pound can bean sprouts, drained
1 small can bamboo sprouts, drained
1 small can water chestnuts

Mix first 4 ingredients for sauce in bowl. Rub suet over chafing dish, skillet or wok until about 2 tablespoons have been realized; remove. Add meats, cooking briskly, turning often, using chopsticks or big spoon or fork. Add vegetables, pour sauce over entire dish. Allow to bubble; turn frequently until cooked down. Serve with hot cooked rice. Serves 4. *This is a happy fun recipe to make with friends. It was published in a Federation of Somans Club cookbook also.*

Nancy J. Hawkins, Barnard-Good House

ITALIAN ROAST BEEF

4 tablespoons shortening
1 (5-pound) rolled rump beef roast
Salt to taste

½ teaspoon freshly ground pepper
1½ to 2 cups dry red wine

Melt shortening in Dutch oven. Cook beef until brown, approximately 10 to 15 minutes. Season with salt and pepper. Pour wine over beef and cover. Cook at 325 degrees for 3 to 3½ hours. Cool and refrigerate, covered for 8 hours. To serve, slice thinly. Serves 10 to 12. *A great picnic or summer dish.*

Jeannie Lukk
Elkton, Maryland

EASY BEEF BOURGUIGNON

5 pounds lean stew beef, cubed
Salt and lemon pepper to taste
3 pounds fresh mushrooms

1 envelope dry onion soup mix
2 (10-ounce) cans cream of
   mushroom soup

Season beef with salt and lemon pepper. Mix with rest ingredients. Put in casserole, cover, and bake at 275 degrees for 4 to 5 hours. Add a splash of sherry before serving (optional). Serves 8 to 10. *A good, easy party dinner that men love.*

Joan Warner

SHERRIED BEEF

3 pounds stewing beef
2 cans cream of mushroom soup

1 envelope onion soup mix
¾ cup sherry

Combine beef, soup and soup mix. Add sherry to beef mixture. Cover and bake at 325 degrees for 3 hours. Serve with noodles or rice. Serves 6.

Tib Lamson

BUTTERFLIED LEG OF LAMB

1 (6 to 7 pounds) leg of lamb,
   butterflied
1 cup dry red wine
½ cup olive oil
2 tablespoons chopped parsley
2 tablespoons chopped chives
1 large onion, chopped

3 garlic cloves, minced
1 teaspoon salt
1 teaspoon Worcestershire
¼ teaspoon freshly ground pepper
⅛ teaspoon marjoram
⅛ teaspoon thyme
⅛ teaspoon rosemary

Place lamb, fat side down in shallow glass container. Combine all other ingredients. Pour over lamb. Refrigerate overnight or at least 4 hours. Grill lamb slowly on open grill, basting with the marinade. Allow approximately 20 minutes per side. Let meat rest 10 minutes before cutting. Slice on a slight diagonal, carve meat in fairly thin slices. Serves 8. *This is great for summer entertaining.*

Rona Craig

RACK OF LAMB MOUTARDE

2 (6 to 8 rib) racks of lamb
1 cup fresh bread crumbs
¼ cup chopped fresh parsley
2 garlic cloves, crushed
½ teaspoon salt

¼ teaspoon cracked pepper
2½ tablespoons Dijon mustard
¼ cup butter, melted
Chopped fresh parsley

Trim off all fat from lamb. Place in a roasting pan, meat side down. Roast at 450 degrees for 15 minutes. Remove and let cool 10 to 15 minutes. Combine crumbs, parsley, garlic, salt and pepper. Spread mustard over top of lamb. Press crumb mixture into mustard, drizzle with butter. Roast another 6 to 8 minutes for medium rare. Garnish with parsley. Serves 4 to 6.

Kristin Hallberg
Virginia Beach, Virginia

LAMB MEATBALLS WITH YOGURT SAUCE

1 (8 ounce) carton plain yogurt
½ cup diced cucumber
1 clove garlic, minced
¼ teaspoon dried dillweed
2 pounds ground lamb
1 cup soft breadcrumbs

⅓ cup chopped almonds
⅓ cup chopped parsley
1 egg, beaten
½ teaspoon salt
½ teaspoon pepper

Combine yogurt, cucumber, garlic and dillweed, mix well. Cover the mixture and refrigerate. Combine remaining ingredients: mix well. Shape into 1 inch balls. Place on greased broiler pan. Bake at 350 degrees for 20 minutes. Serve meatballs with yogurt sauce. Serves 8.

Joanne Heal

MANDARIN PORK AND VEGETABLES

Sauce

2 tablespoons cornstarch
1¼ cups water
⅓ cup soy sauce
⅓ cup dark corn syrup
¼ to ½ teaspoon crushed dried
  red pepper

In bowl mix cornstarch and water until smooth. Add remaining ingredients.

Entree

4 tablespoons oil, divided
1 pound boneless pork, cut in thin
  strips
2 cloves garlic, minced
2 cups broccoli florets and sliced
stems
2 onions, cut in wedges
1 carrot, cut in 2-inch julienne
  strips
½ pound mushrooms, sliced

In large skillet heat 2 tablespoons oil over medium high heat. Add pork and garlic. Stir fry 5 minutes or until tender. Remove from skillet. Heat 2 tablespoons oil. Add broccoli onions and carrots. Stir fry 1 minute or until vegetables are crisp tender. Return pork to skillet. Restir sauce, stir into skillet. Stirring constantly, bring to boil over medium heat and boil 1 minute. Serve over rice. *Variations:* Omit pork, use chicken (stir fry 2 to 3 minutes) or beef (stir fry 1 to 2 minutes). Add with mushrooms: 1 can water chestnuts and/or 4 ounces frozen snow peas (thawed). Serves 4.

Marge Wunder

LOIN OF PORK APRICOT

10 apricots (dried)
½ cup warm water
4 pounds loin of pork
2 teaspoons salt
1 teaspoon pepper
¼ teaspoon ginger
1 small can of apricot juice

Soak apricots in warm water for ½ hour. Drain. Save liquid. Insert apricots deep into pork loin (make slits with knife). Rub meat with salt, pepper and ginger. Place meat in roasting pan. Roast uncovered at 325 degrees for 40 to 45 minutes per pound. Add apricot juice to drippings and taste. Serves 6 to 8. *Tastes terrific with corn pudding souffle!*

Elizabeth von Schlichten

APPLES'N STUFFING PORK CHOPS

6 boneless pork chops (½-inch thick)
1 (22-ounce) can apple pie filling

2 cups bread stuffing mix (unseasoned)

Add to stuffing:
2 tablespoons chopped onions
½ cup chopped celery
⅛ teaspoon pepper

1 beaten egg
¼ cup melted butter
Milk to moisten

Brown chops on both sides and place in 13x9-inch baking dish. Pour pie filling evenly over chops. Divide stuffing into six equal portions-then place a portion on each chop. Cover with tight lid or foil and bake at 325 degrees for 1 hour and 15 minutes. Serves 4 to 6.

Ethel Sowers

SWEET AND SOUR PORK

1 (3¾ pound) pork shoulder
¾ cup flour, divided
1 tablespoon, plus 1 teaspoon ground ginger
½ cup oil
2 (15¼-ounce) cans pineapple chunks, undrained
½ cup vinegar
½ cup soy sauce
½ cup sugar
1 tablespoon Worcestershire sauce

1 tablespoon salt
¾ teaspoon pepper
2 small green peppers, cut into strips
1 (16-ounce) can bean sprouts, drained
1 (8-ounce) can sliced water chestnuts, drained
2 tablespoons chili sauce
Hot cooked rice

Trim fat from pork, and cut meat into 1-inch cubes. Combine ¼ cup flour and ginger and dredge pork in flour mixture. Heat oil in a large Dutch iron oven medium heat; add pork, and cook until browned. Remove pork; drain on paper towels. Drain pineapple, reserving juice; set pineapple aside. Add enough water to pineapple juice to make 2¾ cups; gradually stir into remaining ½ cup flour. Add to Dutch oven; stir well. Add pork, vinegar, and next 5 ingredients. Cover, reduce heat, and simmer 1 hour or until pork is tender, stirring occasionally. Add pineapple chunks, green pepper, bean sprouts, water chestnuts, and chili sauce; cook 5 minutes. Serve over rice. Serves 8 to 10.

Alberta Craig

ZESTY PORK CHOPS

6 pork chops
1 can stewed tomatoes
1 green pepper, sliced rings

1 large onion, sliced thinly
1 lemon, sliced very thinly

In skillet brown chops. Pour tomatoes over and add other ingredients. Cover tightly and bake at 325 degrees for about 1 hour or until tender.

Kathryn L. Lance
Avalon, New Jersey

SHERRIED HAM

1 (8 to 10 pound) ham

½ bottle sherry (not cooking sherry)

Trim ham and make several slits on outside. Place in pot with lid. Pour sherry over ham and cover pot. Cook at 325 degrees for approximately 1½ hours. Serves 8 to 10. *Delicious!*

Ann Tourison

FRIED HAM WITH APPLES

1 slice moist cured ham, ½ inch thick

2 apples, peeled, cored and sliced
½ cup applejack brandy

Warm a heavy skillet over moderate heat and rub with edges of ham slice to coat with fat. Place ham in skillet and cook over medium heat until browned. Turn and brown other side. Remove to warm platter. Pour off all but 1 tablespoon of ham fat. Add apples and applejack. Cook until apples are tender but not mushy. Remove apples. Place on top of ham. Pour warm applejack over dish and serve with hot biscuits. Serves 4.

HOT DOG STEW

2 pounds franks, sliced ½ inch thick
1 medium zucchini quartered and sliced ½ inch thick
1 large green pepper in 1 inch squares

3 ribs celery sliced ½ inch thick
4 pepperoncini left whole
2 (10-ounce) boxes frozen green beans
1 large can tomato sauce

Put all in a large pot (I use a 4 quart Dutch oven). Bring to a boil. Cover and simmer about 30 to 40 minutes. Serves 4 to 6. *I serve this with rice. It's a favorite busy day, or camping dish.*

Pauline Robinson

EASY VEAL MARSALA

6 veal tenders
½ pound mushrooms, sauteed

½ cup Marsala wine

Shake tenders in seasoned flour. Brown in butter and place in casserole with sauteed mushrooms. Add wine to skillet to stir up flour bits. Pour this over the meat. Bake at 350 degrees for 30 minutes. Serves 4. *May be prepared ahead and baked before serving.*

Kathryn L. Lance
Avalon, New Jersey

SPIZZATA

2 pounds cubed veal
½ cup olive oil
4 green peppers, sliced
1 medium onion, sliced

1 can sliced mushrooms
1 (20 ounce) can crushed tomatoes
½ cup white wine or vermouth

Pound meat until ¼-inch thick. In a large frying pan, put ¼ cup oil and saute meat until tender. Remove to a dish and add ¼ cup oil and saute peppers, until tender but not brown. Remove and saute onoin and mushrooms for 5 minutes. Add crushed tomatoes, then add veal, pepper, and wine. Let simmer slowly for 20 to 30 minutes. Salt and pepper to taste. Serves 4.

Janna Brown
Newark, Delaware

VEAL

VEAL WITH SHERRY CREAM SAUCE

1 pound veal cutlets pounded until
    ¼-inch thick
Flour for dredging
¼ cup clarified butter
2 shallots, minced
Pinch of caraway seeds

¼ cup medium dry sherry
¼ cup dry white wine
2 cups heavy cream
1 tablespoon minced fresh parsley
    leaves

Pat the veal dry, season with salt and pepper and dredge in the flour, shaking off the excess. In large heavy skillet heat the clarified butter and in moderate heat add the shallots, stirring 30 seconds. Increase the heat slightly to moderate high and add the veal in batches and the caraway seeds. Brown the veal and as it is done tranfer to a platter. Return veal to skillet, add the sherry and the white wine, and reduce the liquid by half. Add the cream and reduce the liquid over moderate heat until it is thickened slightly. Season with salt and pepper and garnish with Parsley. Serves 4.

Elizabeth von Schlichten

VEAL TAILLEVENT

4 thin slices of veal steak (about
    1½ pounds)
5 tablespoons butter
Flour
Salt

Pepper
2 ounces cognac
¾ cup heavy cream, or sour
    cream
Mushrooms optional

Flour veal steaks lightly and salt and pepper them to taste. Melt butter in large skillet and brown the pieces of meat on both sides over a brisk flame. Reduce heat, and let meat cook slowly until tender, about 20 minutes. Remove meat to a hot platter. Add cognac to juices in pan and flame. Let flame burn out, and take pan off fire for a few minutes. Then add cream to pan and mix it well with the juices. When it comes to the boiling point, let simmer for a few minutes, stirring constantly. Correct seasoning. Pour over steaks and serve very hot. Serves 4.

Katie Gregg

Vegetables
and
Grains

COLONIAL

COLONIAL HOTEL

-JDH-

The Colonial Hotel, 1894
Beach Drive and Ocean Street

A turn of the century advertisement read, "Delight to the surging sea at the most fashionable seaside resort." This surviving Second Empire wooden hotel still captures the Victorian spirit. Its witch-hat turrets and mansard roof are precious reminders of past Cape May.

ALSATIN BRAISED SAUERKRAUT

2 pounds sauerkraut
½ pound bacon
4 tablespoons butter
2 carrots
2 onions
Salt and pepper

¼ cup gin
1 cup dry white wine
2 to 3 cups chicken broth
1 bay leaf
4 parsley sprigs

Drain sauerkraut, soak in cold water ½ hour and squeeze dry. Dice bacon, simmer for 10 minutes. Pat dry. In casserole, saute bacon in butter until lightly brown, add sauerkraut and mix well. Add all other ingredients. Bring to simmer on top of stove. Bake, covered at 325 degrees for 4½ to 5 hours or until liquid is absorbed. Serves 4 to 6.

ASPARAGUS WITH ORANGE HOLLANDAISE SAUCE

1 pound asparagus
¼ cup butter, softened
2 egg yolks
¼ teaspoon finely shredded
  orange peel

1 teaspoon orange juice
Dash salt
Dash pepper
¼ cup dairy sour cream

Place whole spears of asparagus in small amount of water, salted and boiling. Cover pan and cook 10 to 15 minutes, until crisp and tender. Drain well. Divide butter into 3 portions. Combine egg yolks and 1 portion of the butter. Cook and stir over low heat until butter melts. Add another portion. Continue stirring as mixture thickened and butter melts. Add remaining butter stirring constantly. When butter is melted remove from heat. Stir in orange peel, orange juice, salt and pepper. Return to low heat. Cook and stir until thick, 2 to 3 minutes. Remove from heat at once. Blend hot mixture into sour cream and spoon over asparagus. Do not make ahead. Serves 4.

Christi Igoe
Seaville, New Jersey

BEAN CASSEROLE

2 cans pork and beans
1 can butter beans
1 can lima beans, drained
1 can kidney beans, drained
1 pound bacon, browned, diced
1 pound ground beef, browned, drained

1 pound onions, sauteed
½ cup catsup
¼ cup barbecue sauce
1½ tablespoons prepared mustard
2 tablespoons vinegar
½ cup brown sugar

Mix all ingredients and bake at 350 degrees for 1 hour. *Great picnic dish!*

Darlene Orminski

CREOLE GREEN BEANS

6 slices diced bacon
¾ cup chopped onion
¾ cup chopped green pepper
2 tablespoons flour
2 tablespoon brown sugar
1 tablespoon Worcestershire sauce
½ teaspoon salt

¼ teaspoon pepper
⅛ teaspoon dry mustard
1 (16-ounce) can peeled tomatoes
2 cans green beans, drained
Or 2 packages frozen green beans cooked and drained

Cook bacon until crisp, remove from skillet. Add onion and green pepper to 3 tablespoons bacon drippings. Saute until tender. Blend in flour, sugar, Worcestershire sauce, salt, pepper and mustard. Add tomatoes. Cook, stirring constantly, until thickened. Add beans and heat through. Top with bacon. Serves 4 to 6. *Can be made ahead and re-heated but do not add bacon until just before you serve.*

Nancy Wisenauer

HARVARD BEETS

1 (8¼-ounce) can sliced beets
1 tablespoon sugar
1 teaspoon cornstarch

2 tablespoons vinegar
1 tablespoon butter or margarine

Drain beets, reserve ¼ cup liquid. Combine sugar, cornstarch, and ⅛ teaspoon salt (optional). Stir in reserved beet liquid, vinegar and butter. Cook, stirring constantly, until mixture is bubbly. Stir in beets, heat through, about 10 minutes. Serves 2. *Do not make ahead.*

Justine Hammett

BROCCOLI CASSEROLE

5 packages of chopped broccoli
1½ cans cream of celery soup,
   undiluted
36 round buttery
   crackers,crumbled

½ cup margarine or butter
1 cup sharp cheese, shredded

Cook and drain broccoli. Mix with soup. Put in large buttered pyrex baking dish. Arrange cheese on top. Melt margarine or butter and mix in cracker crumbs, and put on top. Bake at 350 degrees for 20 to 30 minutes. If you want to make ½ the recipe, use 3 packages of broccoli. Serves 8 to 10.

Mary Trexler

BROCCOLI MOLD

Broccoli Filling
3 (10-ounce) boxes of frozen
   broccoli, or 3 bundles fresh
   broccoli (3 pounds)
1 teaspoon salt
½ cup grated Parmesan cheese

1 clove garlic, chopped
½ cup finely chopped onion
1½ cups light cream or milk
6 eggs beaten lightly
½ pound prosciutto ham

Oil an 8 cup mold. Set aside. Cook broccoli 15 to 20 minutes until soft. Drain. Puree in blender (Don't over-puree to liquid). To pureed broccoli add: salt, Parmesan cheese, garlic, onion, light cream or milk, and eggs. Stir well. Mixture will resemble a custard. Line oiled mold with overlapping slices of prosciutto. Ladle filling into mold. Sprinkle with grated nutmeg. Fold pieces of prosciutto over filling. Place mold in pan of boiling water (bain marie) and bake at 350 degrees for 25 to 30 minutes. Top should be firm when finished. Allow to set for 15 minutes after it comes out of oven. Loosen sides with a knife and turn out onto serving platter. Garnish with lemon wedges. May serve with a hollandaise or Cheddar sauce if desired. Serves 6 to 8. *A flavorful vegetable which may be prepared a day ahead and held uncooked in refrigerator.*

Bonita Wolchko-Rivera

BROCCOLI SUPREME

1 egg, slightly beaten
1 (10-ounce) package frozen
  broccoli, partly thawed
1 (8½-ounce) can creamed corn

1 tablespoon grated onion
Dash of salt and pepper
3 tablespoons butter
¾ cup croutons or stuffing mix

Combine egg, broccoli, corn, onion, salt and pepper in an ungreased casserole dish. In a small pan melt butter. Add croutons and toss to coat. Add to casserole. Bake, uncovered, at 350 for 35 minutes. Serves 4 to 6.

Julie Merson

MARINATED CARROT STICKS

8 small carrots, cut into sticks
3 tablespoons vinegar
3 tablespoons oil
1 small garlic clove, crushed

¾ teaspoon seasoned salt
¼ teaspoon salt
Minced parsley

Place cut carrot sticks in shallow dish. Mix other ingredients, except parsley, and pour over carrots. Cover tightly and refrigerate overnight, turning sticks occasionally. Drain, arrange sticks and sprinkle with parsley. Serves 4. *Easy and very tasty.*

Jan Wood, Woodleigh House

AUNT BETTINA'S CARROTS

2 pounds carrots (smaller the
  better) cut in bite-sized pieces
  and cooked 20 minutes
1 can tomato soup, undiluted
¾ cup sugar
½ cup vinegar

½ cup oil
1 teaspoon salt
½ teaspoon prepared mustard
1 green pepper, diced
3 small onions

Combine the ingredients. Mix thoroughly. Marinate 24 hours. Serve hot or cold. Serves 6 to 8.

Donna Gaver Shank
Dover, Delaware

MASHED (SMASHED) CARROTS

2 pounds large California carrots
8 ounces sour cream

1 tablespoon light brown sugar
2 tablespoons brandy or sherry

Peel carrots and cut in small pieces. Place in large saucepan with enough water to cover. Cook for tenderness (20 to 30 minutes). Drain well. In same saucepan mash carrots until smooth texture. Add brown sugar, sour cream and brandy or sherry. Mix well. Reheat to blend. Place in covered casserole (to reheat later if desired) at 350 degrees for 20 minutes. Serves 8. *A family recipe I serve at the holidays with turkey or ham. Great for color. Even guests who do not like carrots enjoy this "surprise."*

Pat Trumbull

HUNTINGTON CORN PUDDING

9 whole eggs
2 cups half cream and half milk
(half-and-half)
2 pounds ground or crushed corn
(canned is ok)

1¼ cups sugar
½ cup cornstarch
¼ cup butter

Beat eggs and whip with half-and-half until light and fluffy. Add corn, sugar, cornstarch and butter. Blend well. Pour into lightly greased 12x8-inch pan. Elevate pan in tray half filled with water. Bake at 350 degrees. Serve warm. Serves 6. *Especially good with buffet night. Does nicely with a very dry Chablis.*

George Hinkle, The Huntington House

COUNTRY STYLE CORN PUDDING

1 (15-ounce) can whole kernel corn,
drained
1 (15-ounce) can cream style corn
2 eggs, slightly beaten

½ cup margarine, melted
1 cup sour cream
1 (8½-ounce) package of corn
muffin mix

Mix together all ingredients. Pour into ungreased 12x8-inch or 13x9-inch pan. Bake at 350 degrees for 40 to 45 minutes. Allow to cool slightly before cutting. Cut into 8 to 12 pieces and serve. Serves 8 to 12.

O'Nile Stalnaker

EGGPLANT CASSEROLE

2 medium eggplants (about 2½
   pounds) peeled and cubed
2 cups chopped onions
1 (28-ounce) can tomatoes, well
   drained, juice reserved
1 teaspoon salt
½ teaspoon pepper
2 tablespoons Worcestershire
   sauce

½ cup thick cream sauce (see
   recipe below)
¼ cup plus 1 tablespoon butter or
   margarine
½ cup bread crumbs
½ cup shredded Cheddar cheese
Paprika

Place eggplant and onions in large pan with water barely to cover; simmer until tender, 5 to 7 minutes. Drain well. Add tomatoes (reserve juice for cream sauce), salt and pepper, Worcestershire sauce, cream and ¼ cup butter. Melt remaining tablespoon of butter in an 8-cup baking dish; sprinkle bottom with ¼ cup bread crumbs. Add eggplant mixture, sprinkle top with cheese, remaining bread crumbs and paprika. Bake at 350 degrees for 10 to 15 minutes or until heated through. Serves 6 to 8. *This is one of Helen's most loved recipes. The bowl is always empty.*

Thick Cream Sauce
1½ tablespoons butter or
   margarine
2 tablespoons flour

½ cup milk or juice from tomatoes

Melt butter in saucepan. Add flour and cook over low heat until well blended. Add liquid and cook until thickened.

Helen Dickerson, The Chalfonte Hotel

EGGPLANT CREOLE

1 large green pepper, diced and
   sauteed in bacon fat
1 large onion, sliced
1 (16-ounce) can tomatoes
1 (8-ounce) can tomato sauce
1 medium to large eggplant,
   peeled and cut into 1-inch square
   pieces and added to above

3 strips bacon, crisp
1 scant teaspoon salt
Other seasonings optional

Simmer vegetables for about 15 to 20 minutes. Add bacon pieces. Shred
Cheddar cheese on top. Bread crumbs may also be added to top. Bake at
350 degrees for ½ hour. May also add zucchini, parsley and canned tuna for
main dish casserole. Serves 6.

Jean Anne Christie
Wayne, New Jersey

MUSHROOM CASSEROLE

6 slices white bread
4 tablespoons butter
1 pound mushrooms, sliced
1 cup onions, chopped
1 cup green pepper, chopped
1 cup mayonnaise
¾ teaspoon salt

Pepper to taste
1½ cups milk
2 eggs, beaten
1 can mushroom soup
¾ cup saltines, crushed
½ cup mozzarella cheese,
   shredded

Butter the bread and cut into cubes. Saute mushrooms, add the onions,
peppers, mayonnaise, salt and pepper, and cook for 5 minutes. In a 2 quart
buttered casserole spread a layer of half the bread, then a layer of
mushroom mixture, and then a layer of the remaining bread. Over all pour
the milk and eggs beaten together. Chill for 1 hour. Spread the undiluted
can of mushroom soup over all, then a layer of the saltines. Last, cover
with mozzarella cheese. Bake at 350 degrees for 1 hour. Serves 4 to 6. *Add
a standing rib roast, and broccoli lightly sauteed in sesame oil.*

Helenclare Leary

MUSHROOMS FLORENTINE

1 pound fresh mushrooms, sliced
2 (10-ounce) packages frozen
   spinach
1 teaspoon salt

½ cup chopped onions
¼ cup melted butter
1 cup shredded Cheddar cheese
Touch of garlic salt

Saute mushrooms until brown. Line a shallow 10-inch casserole with cooked spinach which has been seasoned with salt, chopped onions and melted butter. Sprinkle with ½ cup Cheddar cheese. Arrange sauteed mushrooms on spinach. Season with garlic salt. Cover with remaining cheese. Bake at 350 degrees for 20 minutes. Serves 6. *May be prepared in advance.*

Dorothy Louise Bond
Drexel Hill, Pennsylvania

LIMA BEAN CASSEROLE

2 cups dried lima beans (large)
1 medium can tomatoes, drained
2 sweet pickles, chopped
1 onion, chopped

1 package pasteurized processed
   cheese spread, (small size)
   chopped in cubes
Salt and pepper to taste

Soak beans overnight. Cook until soft. Drain. Add tomatoes, pickles, onion, cubed cheese, and seasoning. Place in greased casserole and bake at 325 degrees for 45 minutes. This is an old family recipe-always popular at picnics and pot luck suppers. Serves 6 to 8. *I have found a short cut by using pre-cooked lima beans (1 medium can and 4 small cans drained) and 1 large can tomatoes.*

Fran McDougal

PEAS VINAIGRETTE

2 packages petit frozen peas
½ cup oil
3 tablespoons vinegar
2 tablespoons sweet pickles, finely
   chopped

1 tablespoon diced pimientos
1 teaspoon salt
½ teaspoon pepper

Cook peas by pouring one or two kettles of boiling water over them. Mix remaining ingredients well. Pour over peas. Refrigerate at least 2 hours. Toss lightly with a fork before serving. Serves 6 to 8.

Karen Andrus

MAKE AHEAD MASHED POTATOES

3 pounds medium size potatoes,
   pared (about 9)
1½ cups dairy sour cream
¼ cup butter or margarine
1½ teaspoons salt

¼ teaspoon pepper
¼ cup packaged bread crumbs
1 tablespoon butter or margarine,
   melted

Cook potatoes until tender. Drain thoroughly. Combine potatoes, sour cream, butter, salt and pepper in large bowl. Beat at low speed with electric mixer until blended. Beat at high speed until light and fluffy. Pile lightly into a buttered 2-quart casserole. Cover and refrigerate overnight, if desired. Bake, covered, at 325 degrees for 1 hour. Toss bread crumbs in melted butter. Sprinkle over potatoes. Continue baking, uncovered, 30 minutes. Serves 6 to 8.

Mary Trexler

HOLIDAY POTATO DISH

4 pounds unpared potatoes, cooked and drained
1 cup chopped onion
¼ cup butter
1 can cream of celery soup
1 pint dairy sour cream

1½ cups shredded Cheddar cheese
½ cup crushed corn flakes
3 tablespoons melted butter
Pimiento strips
Fresh parsley, chopped

Remove skins from potatoes; shred into bowl. Saute onion in ¼ cup melted butter until tender. Remove from heat. Stir in soup and sour cream. Pour over potatoes and cheese; mix well. Turn into greased 13x9x2-inch baking dish. Cover and refrigerate overnight. Sprinkle with corn flakes, drizzle with 3 tablespoons butter. Bake at 350 degrees for one hour. Garnish with pimiento and parsley. Serves 6 to 8.

Julie Merson

SECOND TIME MASHED POTATOES
(OR POTATO CAKES)

1½ cups leftover mashed potatoes
1 egg
¼ cup milk
Bacon bits (small handful)

Shredded Cheddar cheese or chunks of pasteurized processed cheese
Frying pan
1 teaspoon oil or margarine

Mix egg, milk, bacon and cheese with mashed potatoes. Take ¼ of mixture, form into patty and fry in skillet. (All four can be done at once, like pancakes). Fry until light brown on both sides. Serves 4. *An easy old family recipes.*

Christy Igoe
Seaville, New Jersey

MASHED POTATO ZUCCHINI CASSEROLE

3 tablespoons butter, divided
2 tablespoons packaged dry bread crumbs
4 to 5 small potatoes
1 cup shredded zucchini
½ cup chopped onion
½ teaspoon dried dillweed
1 tablespoon flour
½ teaspoon salt
⅛ teaspoon pepper
½ cup milk
2 eggs, separated
1 cup shredded Gruyere or Swiss cheese

Butter casserole with 1 tablespoon butter. Sprinkle evenly with bread crumbs. Cook potatoes in 1-inch boiling water until tender. Drain. Remove skins. In a medium bowl beat potatoes with electric mixer until smooth. In a medium pan melt 2 tablespoons butter, zucchini, onion and dillweed and cook until vegetables are tender. Stir in flour, salt and pepper. Cook 1 to 2 minutes, stirring constantly. Remove from heat. Gradually stir in milk and cook until mixture boils and thickens. Beat mixture into mashed potatoes. Beat in egg yolks and cheese. Beat the egg whites until stiff but not dry and gently fold into the potato mixture. Spoon into the prepared casserole. Bake at 375 degrees for 20 to 25 minutes, or until puffed and lightly browned. Serves 4.

Kathryn Gregg

SHERRIED SWEET POTATO CASSEROLE

3 (18-ounce) cans sweet potatoes (or cooked fresh)
1 cup brown sugar
2 tablespoons cornstarch
½ teaspoon salt
1 teaspoon grated orange peel
2 cups orange juice
½ cup raisins
6 tablespoons butter
⅓ cup sherry
¼ cup chopped walnuts

Cut potatoes in ½-inch thick slices and arrange in 13x8x1-inch baking dish. Sprinkle with little salt (if desired). In saucepan combine brown sugar, cornstarch and ½ teaspoon salt. Blend in orange juice and peel; add raisins. Cook and stir over medium heat until thick and bubbly; cook 1 minute more. Add butter, sherry and walnuts. Stir until butter melts. Pour over potatoes. Bake at 325 degrees for 30 minutes or until potatoes are well glazed, basting occasionally. Serves 8 to 10.

Sally Sachs

OVEN-CRISP POTATOES

6 to 8 potatoes, peeled and
    quartered
4 tablespoons olive oil

2 tablespoons flour
Salt and pepper

Parboil potatoes for 5 minutes. Toss with remaining ingredients in a baking dish. Arrange in single layer. Bake at 425 degrees for 35 to 45 minutes. Serves 6 to 8.

SPINACH ARTICHOKE CASSEROLE

3 packages frozen chopped
    spinach
2 jars marinated artichoke hearts
8 ounces sour cream

3 tablespoons butter
⅔ package leek soup mix
Salt and pepper to taste
½ package herbed stuffing mix

Cook spinach, drain well, removing as much water as possible. Mix sour cream and soup mix, add spinach, salt and pepper. Drain artichoke hearts, cut in pieces, and place in bottom of flat casserole. Spread mixture over artichokes. Top with stuffing. Bake at 350 degrees for 1 hour.

SPINACH AND ARTICHOKE BAKE

3 packages frozen chopped
    spinach
1 can artichoke hearts
1 (8-ounce) package cream cheese

2 tablespoons mayonnaise
6 tablespoons milk
Romano or Parmesan cheese,
    grated

Drain spinach completely. cut artichoke hearts in half and place in bottom of a greased casserole. Place spinach on top. Mix cream cheese, mayonnaise and milk in mixer. Pour over casserole, covering all the spinach. Sprinkle cheese over top. Bake at 350 degrees for 25 to 30 minutes or until heated thoroughly. Serves 6 to 8.

SPINACH CASSEROLE

2 or 3 packages chopped frozen
  spinach
Butter to taste
Salt to taste
Nutmeg to taste
1 can artichoke hearts
  (non-marinated)

1 can sliced water chestnuts
1 (8-ounce) package cream cheese
¾ cup packaged dressing mix
Parmesan cheese or French fried
  onions to cover

Cook and drain spinach. Add butter, salt and nutmeg. Place in 2 to 3-quart casserole. Cut each artichoke heart in half and layer over spinach. Layer water chestnuts over artichoke hearts. Dot with butter. Soften cream cheese with a little milk and spread over all. Brown dressing mix in skillet with butter, and spread over top. Add either Parmesan cheese or French fried onions. Bake at 325 degrees until warmed through, not more than ½ hour. Serves 4 to 6. *Excellent with filet mignon, roast beef, etc.*

Anita M. Laird

GEOFF AND BOBBIE'S SPINACH TERRIFIC

2 packages frozen spinach
½ cup chopped onion
½ cup margarine

1 can artichokes (water pack)
1 cup sour cream
½ cup Parmesan cheese

Cook spinach. Drain. Saute onion in margarine. chop artichokes. Mix all together. Put in baking dish and bake at 350 degrees for 30 minutes (longer if deep dish is use). Serves 4 to 6. *An incredibly easy dish from superb cooks.*

Donna Gaver Shank
Dover, Delaware

SPINACH CASSEROLE

4 boxes chopped frozen spinach
2 tablespoons chopped onions
1 cup tomato sauce
2 cups sour cream
1 cup sliced mushrooms

2 cups sharp cheese, shredded
(about 1 pound)
½ cup crumbs browned in 1
tablespoon butter

Cook spinach. Add onions and drain thoroughly. Stir in tomato sauce, sour cream, mushrooms and cheese. Just before baking top with buttered crumbs. Bake, uncovered, in 12x8-inch shallow baking dish, or 2-quart casserole at 350 degrees for 45 minutes. Serves 8.

Lydia M. Magee, Belmont Guest House

GREEN TOMATO PIE

1⅔ cups sugar
3 tablespoons flour
3½ cups thinly sliced green
   tomatoes

3 tablespoons grated lemon rind
¼ teaspoon salt
¼ cup butter
Pastry for 2 crust pie

Combine the sugar and flour in a bowl and stir in remaining ingredients, except butter and pastry. Place in pastry-lined pie pan and dot with butter. Add the top crust and cut slits in center. Bake at 450 degrees for 10 minutes. Reduce temperature to 350 degrees and bake for 30 minutes longer. Serve with wedges of cheese. Serves 4 to 6.

Christy Igoe
Seaville, New Jersey

TURNIP-POTATO PATTIES

⅓ cup turnips, peeled and cubed
1 cup potatoes, peeled and cubed
2½ scallions, finely sliced
1 egg, lightly beaten
¼ cup flour

Oil for frying
Fresh parsley sprigs for garnish
3 tablespoons mayonnaise
1 teaspoon bottled horseradish,
 drained

In large saucepan boil the turnip and potato cubes for 15 to 17 minutes, or until tender, and drain. Mash together in a bowl and stir in the scallions, egg, flour, salt and pepper to taste. In large heavy skillet heat ½-inch of the oil to 360 degrees. Spoon in mounds of the mixture, flattening them into
patties. Fry them until golden brown (about 4 minutes), turning once. Drain on paper towel. Combine in small bowl the mayonnaise and horseradish sauce. Serve with patties, garnish with parsley. Serves two for brunch, or as a light dinner entree. *Sausages make a nice accompaniment.*

Elizabeth von Schlichten

TURNIP ROAST

4 cups yellow turnips, mashed
 and cooked
3 tablespoons melted butter
1 egg, beaten

¼ cup parsley, chopped
½ cup Parmesan cheese, grated,
 or bread crumbs (optional)

Mix together first four ingredients and put into a baking dish. Sprinkle cheese or bread crumbs on top if desired. Bake at 350 degrees for 20 minutes. Serves 4 to 6.

Betty Lindsey
Neptune Beach, Florida

VEGETABLE STIR FRY

2 bunches broccoli
4 medium carrots
1 head cauliflower (I used about
   ½)

1 bunch (about 6 or 8) green
   onions, chopped
1 tablespoon oil

Clean all vegetables and cut broccoli and cauliflower tops off. Cut carrots in
thin strips about 2-inchs long. Not more than 10 minutes before dinner is to
be served, in large skillet, heat oil (medium high heat), and vegetables,
stirring constantly for 5 to 8 minutes. Serve immediately. Serves 6 to 8.
The object is that vegetables are to be only heated, not cooked until soft.
Veggies done right will be crunchy but hot. Try adding snow peas.

Christy Igoe
Seaville, New Jersey

MIXED VEGETABLE CASSEROLE

1 package frozen peas
1 package frozen string beans
1 package frozen baby lima beans
2 green peppers

½ pint whipping cream
1⅓ cups mayonnaise
¾ cups grated Parmesan cheese

Cook vegetables and season to taste. Whip cream. Combine with
mayonnaise and cheese. Layer vegetables in 2-quart buttered casserole.
Pour sauce over all. Bake at 350 degrees for 30 minutes. Serves 10 to 12.

Jessie Lisk

156

CALIFORNIA VEGETABLE MEDLEY

2 large Italian zucchini
1 red bell pepper
1 green bell pepper
1 onion cut in very thin slices
  lengthwise
1 cup corn

2 ripe tomatoes, diced
1 cup shredded Cheddar cheese
2 tablespoons olive oil
1½ teaspoons Lowry's® "Pinch of
  Herbs"

Slice zucchini in rounds about ⅛-inch thick. Slice bell peppers in strips. In wok or frying pan put olive oil. Then hot stir fry zucchini and onion for 1 minute. Add peppers and continue stir frying 1 minute more. Add corn and tomatoes. Stir gently. Remove from wok and put in 8x8-inch pan. Sprinkle with "Pinch of Herbs" and cheese. Cover and bake at 350 degrees for 20 to 25 minutes.

Marcia Hammett
Camarilla, California

VEGETABLE STRATA

1 (16-ounce) package frozen
  broccoli, cauliflower and carrots
6 slices white bread, cut into
  ½-inch cubes
1 cup chopped cooked ham
8 eggs

1½ cups milk
1 teaspoon dry mustard
½ teaspoon garlic powder
½ teaspoon onion powder
6 ounces (1½ cups) shredded
  Chedder cheese

Grease 13x9-inch (3-quart) baking dish. Arrange frozen vegetables in bottom of prepared dish; Sprinkle with bread cubes and ham (layered). In medium bowl, combine eggs milk, mustard, garlic powder and onion powder, mix well. Pour egg mixture over vegetables; sprinkle with cheese. Cover with plastic wrap. Refrigerate 6 hours or overnight. Heat oven to 350 degrees. Bake vegetable strata, uncovered, at 350 degrees for 40 to 45 minutes or until knife inserted near center comes out clean. Serves 6. *Variation:* Use chicken, shrimp, crabmeat as substitute for ham.

Rosemary Hartman

VEGETABLE LASAGNA
A Great Microwave Dish

8 ounces fresh mushrooms, chopped
1 green pepper, chopped
1 medium onion, chopped
1 clove garlic, minced
2 tablespoons olive oil
1 (16-ounce) can whole tomatoes, broken up
1 (12-ounce) can tomato paste
⅓ cup red wine, or water
1 tablespoon parsley flakes
1½ teaspoons salt (optional)
2 teaspoons sugar
1 teaspoon basil leaves
1 teaspoon oregano leaves
2 bay leaves
10 ounces ricotta cheese
2 eggs
¼ cup Parmesan cheese
½ teaspoon salt (optional)
¼ teaspoon black pepper
3 cups mozzarella cheese

Combine vegetables in 3-quart bowl with 2 tablespoons water. Cover. Cook in microwave oven 6 to 8 minutes on High until tender. Stir once. Drain and stir in tomatoes, tomato paste, red wine or water, parsley flakes, salt, sugar, basil, oregano and bay leaves. Cook (micro) on High, uncovered, 5 minutes. Stir. Reduce to 50% (Medium) power. Micro 30 minutes until flavors blend and juice thickens. Stir 2 or 3 times. Remove bay leaves. Mix together in medium-size bowl ricotta cheese, eggs, Parmesan, salt and black pepper. Cook 9 lasagna noodles. Grate 3 cups mozzarella cheese. In 12x8-inch pyrex casserole, layer ⅓ noodles, ⅓ ricotta mix, ⅓ sauce and 1 cup cheese. Repeat layers 2 more times. Sprinkle with ¼ cup Parmesan. Micro 50%, 20 minutes until hot and bubbly. Rotate dish ½ turn. Let stand 12 minutes. Serves 8. *Instead of 8 ounces mushrooms, use 3 ounces and add about 2 cups of broccoli florets, sliced carrots, and celery, whatever vegetables are preferred.*

Lynda Leaming
Orange, California

ZUCCHINI PIE

3 cups zucchini, cubed
2 onions, finely chopped
¾ cup grated Romano cheese
1 cup buttermilk biscuit baking
   mix

4 eggs
½ cup oil
1 teaspoon salt
½ teaspoon pepper
1 teaspoon marjoram

Mix all ingredients together in a greased oblong or square casserole. Bake at 350 degrees for 35 to 40 minutes. Serves 4 to 8. *Easy, can be made ahead and frozen.*

Jaye Guarini
Jax, Florida

ZUCCHINI SOUFFLE

2 pounds sliced zucchini
½ cup chopped onions
2 tablespoons butter
1 egg, beaten lightly

2 slices bread, cubed
½ cup mild Cheddar cheese,
   cubed
2 tablespoons butter

Boil zucchini until tender. Drain and set aside. Saute onion in 2 tablespoons of butter. Put into a 2-quart casserole. Add squash, egg, bread, and cheese. Season to taste. Stir to mix and drizzle with butter. Bake at 325 degrees for 30 minutes. Serves 4 to 5.

Mary Kosak

NEW YEAR'S DAY BLACK-EYED PEAS

1¼ cups dried black-eyed peas
1½ quarts water
2 ounces olive oil
1 large onion, chopped
½ green pepper, chopped
1 garlic clove, minced
1 ham or smoked pork hock

1 bay leaf
1 clove
1¼ teaspoons chili powder
Dash Worcestershire
Dash hot pepper sauce
Salt and pepper to taste

Soak peas in water for 24 hours. Drain. In oil, saute onions, celery, peppers and garlic until limp. Place peas and water in large rpasting pan. Add vegetables and remaining ingredients. Cover and bake at 300 degrees for 1 hour. Reduce heat to 275 degrees and bake 4 to 5 hours or until peas are tender. Serves 8 to 10. *Great for holiday buffet and good luck for the New Year!*

Alberta Craig

SAVANNAH RED RICE

¼ pound bacon
½ cup chopped onion
2 cups raw rice
2 cups tomatoes, chopped

½ teaspoon salt
¼ teaspoon pepper
⅛ teaspoon Tabasco

Fry bacon until crisp. Drain. Cook onions in bacon fat until tender. Add washed rice, seasonings, tomatoes and crumbled bacon. Cook over low heat about 10 minutes then pour into 1-quart casserole and cover tightly. Bake at 350 degrees for 1 hour stirring several times. Serves 6 to 8.

GREEN RICE

1 cup raw rice
1 (10-ounce) package frozen
    chopped broccoli
1 medium onion, chopped
2 tablespoons butter

½ cup milk
1 can cream of chicken soup
½ jar pasterized processed cheese
    spread

Cook rice according to directions. Thaw broccoli and fry with onion in butter until tender. Add milk and soup. Heat slowly 10 to 15 minutes. Add cooked rice and cheese spread. Mix thoroughly and heat. Serve immediately. Serves 4 to 6.

Betsy Sands
Malvern, Pennsylvania

RICE CASSEROLE

1 cup converted rice
1 (10-ounce) can beef bouillon
   undiluted

1 (10-ounce) can onion soup
   undiluted

Mix all ingredients in greased casserole and bake at 350 degrees for 1 hour or longer. Serves 6 to 8.

Mary Trexler

Accompaniments

The Eldridge Johnson House ca 1882
33 Perry Street

Locally known as the Pink House, this building reminds one of
a beautifully decorated wedding cake. This is a lavish example
of Cape May gingerbread, in an Italianate/Gothic Revival
house.

APPLE ONION SAUCE

2 tablespoons butter
1 large onion, peeled and sliced
3 apples, peeled, cored and sliced
6 to 8 prunes, snipped in quarters
½ teaspoon cinnamon

¼ teaspoon ginger
Salt to taste
¼ cup applejack or apple juice
1 tablespoon cider vinegar

Heat butter in medium saucepan. Add onion and cook until translucent, but not brown. Add apples, prunes, cinnamon, ginger and salt. Mix well and add the applejack. Cover and simmer for 20 to 30 minutes or until apples are tender but not mushy. Add vinegar and stir well. Cook a minute or two longer. Serves 4. *A fruity side dish that makes pork, ham, duck, and chicken special.*

BAKED PINEAPPLE

½ cup butter
1 cup sugar
3 eggs, beaten

4 cups dry bread cubes
1 cup milk
1 (20-ounce) can crushed pineapple

Cream butter and sugar. Add eggs and blend. Mix the remainder of the ingredients with first mixture. Bake in a greased 12x8-inch baking dish at 350 degrees for 1 hour. Serves 4 to 6. *Easy and good. Good accompaniment with ham. Also a great "one disher" to go to a covered dish supper.*

Lucy Henry
Montgomery, Pennsylvania

BEACH PLUM JELLY

On a cool, clear, breezy late August day with arms and legs well-covered (against bugs) proceed to Higbees Beach. High in the dunes search for Beach Plum bushes where the berries have ripened to dark red or bluish purple. Pick until weary. Bring home and wash the berries. Pour into large pot - add just enough water to show through berries. Cook until soft. Drain and strain through fine sieve. Measure juice and follow recipe for plum jelly on packaged fruit pectin instruction sheet. (Extra beach plum juice may be frozen until needed. The tangy jelly is worth the effort - makes great gifts.

K. C. Bennett

BEECHMONT GRANOLA

1 cup peanut or safflower oil
½ cup honey
½ cup molasses
1 teaspoon vanilla
1½ teaspoons cinnamon
½ teaspoon nutmeg
¼ teaspoon allspice
¼ teaspoon ground cloves

5 cups rolled oats
¼ cup wheat germ
1½ cups unsweetened, shredded
   coconut
1 cup slivered blanched almonds
¾ cup raw sunflower meat
2½ cups mixed, dried fruit

Preheat oven to 350 degrees. In small saucepan combine first eight ingredients and heat over medium heat until honey and molasses have become thin. Mixture should be hot but not boiling. In large bowl, while heating syrup, combine the rest of the ingredients, except fruit. Pour hot liquid
over dry ingredients and mix thoroughly. Using a non-stick cookie sheet,
spread with approximately ½ of the granola mixture (you want a fairly thin
layer). Bake, stirring every 10 minutes. Granola may take up to 40 minutes;
it should be a medium dark brown. Remove from over and place in large
bowl. Repeat with remaining uncooked granola. When all granola is cool,
mix in fruit. Store in air-tight container. Yields about 2½ quarts. *Granola
can be frozen or refrigerated without affecting the taste. Granola is excellent when topped with a Bavarian yogurt called "Quark."*

Heidi J. Hormel
Hanover, Pennsylvani

QUARK
Accompanies Granola

2 cups plain yogurt
½ cup sour cream
Sugar to taste

Cinnamon to taste
Nutmeg to taste
Vanilla to taste

Mix above ingredients together then chill. Yield about 2½ cups. *Top
granola-yum.*

Heidi J. Hormel
Hanover, Pennsylvania

PINEAPPLE PUDDING

5 slices of white cubed bread
4 eggs
1 can crushed pineapple

1 cup sugar
6 tablespoons butter

Drain pineapple. Beat eggs and mix all together in 1½-quart casserole. Bake at 350 degrees for 1 hour. *Delicious as vegetable hot. Delicious as dessert served cold. Great with ham dinner.*

Ann Taylor, Horatio Church House

CHICKEN BARBEQUE SAUCE

¼ cup margarine
½ cup vinegar
1½ cups sherry
½ cup catsup
2 tablespoons Worcestershire
   sauce
Juice of 1 lemon
1 tablespoon dry mustard

2 tablespoons chili powder
1 teaspoon salt
1 teaspoon pepper
¼ cup sugar
2 crushed bay leaves
Pinch cayenne pepper
2 garlic cloves, minced
1 large onion, grated

Melt margarine and add 5 liquid ingredients. Mix dry ingredients and add to liquid. Cook 10 minutes. Brush on chicken that has been coated with olive oil. Yields 2½ cups. *This can be made ahead and stored in the refrigerator.*

Fran McDougal

BACON SCALLION DRESSING

2 tablespoons white vinegar
   (wine)
1 teaspoon bottle horseradish
1 scallion, chopped

3 slices of crisp bacon, drained
   and crumbled
⅓ to ½ cup oil, or to taste

In blender mix the vinegar, horseradish, scallion, bacon, scraping down the sides with a rubber spatula until mixture is smooth. With the motor running add oil in a stream and blend until emulsified. Yield ½ cup.

Eilizabeth von Schlichten

CRANBERRY WINE JELLY

2 cups cranberry juice cocktail
3½ cups sugar

1 pouch (½ package) liquid fruit
    pectin
1 cup sherry wine

Wash canning jars in hot soapy water. Rinse. Put jars in a kettle. Add hot water. Boil 10 minutes. Leave in water until ready to cook jelly. Combine cranberry juice cocktail and sugar in a kettle. Bring to a full rolling boil, stirring constantly. Stir in pectin. Return to full rolling boil. Boil hard for 1 minute. Remove from heat. Stir in wine. Skim off foam. Ladle into hot sterilized jars, leaving ⅛-inch head space. Cap. Good with cold meats. Yields 5 half pints.

Mrs. Lloyd Lisk
Springfield, Pennsylvania

CRISPY PICKLE SLICES

4 quarts young cucumbers,
    unpeeled and thinly sliced
6 medium onions, thinly sliced
2 green peppers, thinly sliced
2 cloves garlic
⅓ cup granulated pickling salt

Ice cubes
4½ cups sugar
3 cups cider vinegar
1½ teaspoons turmeric
1½ teaspoons celery seed
2 tablespoons mustard seed

Combine cucumbers, onions, peppers and whole garlic cloves in a large bowl. Sprinkle with pickling salt. Cover with ice. Mix thoroughly, let stand 3 hours. Drain well and remove garlic. Place in 4 quart pot. Combine remaining ingredients and pour over cucumber mixture. Bring to a boil. Fill 8 pint-size canning jars, that have been scalded, to within ½-inch of the top. Put lids on properly. Place in kettle of boiling water and boil 5 minutes after water returns to a boil. Let jars cool and then secure lids on tightly. Yields 8 pints.

Lannie Ralph
Laurel, Delaware

DILL SAUCE

1 cup salad dressing
1 cup dairy sour cream
½ cup milk

¼ cup chopped dill pickle
¼ cup green onion slices
½ teaspoon dry mustard

Combine and mix well. Yields 3 cups. *Very good as a salad dressing or vegetable topper.*

Christy Igoe
Seaville, New Jersey

GARLIC MINT DRESSING

1 garlic clove
2 tablespoons fresh lime juice
1 teaspoon Dijon style mustard
½ teaspoon dried mint

⅛ teaspoon sugar
¼ teaspoon salt
⅓ cup oil

In blender mix the garlic, lime juice, mustard, mint, sugar, salt. scraping down the sides with a rubber spatula until mixture is smooth. With the motor running add oil in a stream and blend until emulsified. Yields ½ cup.

Elizabeth von Schlichten

GERMAN PUDDING SAUCE

½ cup Marsala wine
2 teaspoons fresh lemon juice

¼ cup sugar
3 egg yolks, beaten

Combine Marsala, lemon juice and sugar in medium-sized sauce pan over low heat. Cook until sugar is dissolved. Pour ½ of hot mixture into beaten yolks, whisking constantly. Return mixtrue to saucepan, cook over low heat, whisking briskly until well thickened and highly frothed. Serve warm over puddings and cakes. Yield 1 cup. *Versatile, rich sauce.*

Mary Suzanne Roehm
Grosse Pointe Woods, Michigan

HOLLANDAISE SAUCE

3 egg yolks
2 tablespoons lemon juice
1 tablespoon water

½ teaspoon salt
Dash of hot pepper sauce
½ cup melted butter

Put egg yolks, lemon juice, water, salt and hot pepper sauce in the blender. Switch blender on and off to mix. Then turn on low and slowly pour in melted butter until mixture emulsifies and thickens. Do not overheat before serving. Yields 1 cup. *This uncooked sauce is almost foolproof and can be made ahead. When heating, make sure not to cook.*

HOT FUDGE SAUCE

¼ cup butter
4 ounces unsweetened chocolate
3 cups sugar

½ teaspoon salt
1 can evaporated milk

Melt butter in double boiler. Add chocolate, then sugar. Mix well. Add salt, stir in milk slowly. Cook 30 minutes, stirring several times. Serve hot over ice cream. Yields 3 cups.

HOT MUSTARD

1 cup dry mustard
1 cup vinegar
2 eggs, well beaten

1 cup sugar
½ teaspoon salt

Mix mustard and vinegar. Let stand overnight. In a saucepan, put well beaten eggs, sugar, and salt. Heat. Add mustard mixture and stir until thickened. Yields 2 cups. *This makes a nice food gift.*

Eloise Bricker
Wilmington, Delaware

ICE BOX CUCUMBER PICKLES

7 cups thin sliced cucumbers
1 cup thin sliced onions
1 cup thin sliced bell peppers
1 teaspoon celery seed

2 tablespoons salt
1 cup vinegar
2 cups sugar

Sprinkle salt, celery seed and sugar on vegetables. Mix well. Add vinegar and mix well. Let set 20 minutes or longer. Yields 5 pints. *Put in sterilized jars and keep in refrigerator.*

Abby Vercoe
Atlantic Beach, Florida

JEZEBEL'S SAUCE

1 (18-ounce) jar pineapple jelly
1 (18-ounce) jar apple jelly
1 (5-ounce) jar horseradish

1 tablespoon freshly ground
  pepper
1 small can dry mustard

Mix all ingredients by hand. Yield 1 quart that keeps indefinitely in refrigerator. *Excellent with ham.*

LEMON BUTTER

3 lemons
2 cups sugar

4 eggs, separated
1 heaping tablespoon butter

Grate rind of one lemon, add juice of 3 lemons, sugar and butter. Put all in pan, add well beaten egg yolks, put on stove. Let come to boil. Have whites well beaten. Add beaten egg whites, beating constantly. Remove from heat as soon as whites are mixed. Set to cool. Yields 1½ cups.

Florence Heal

LEMON SAUCE
From Original Mac Cookbook

2 tablespoons cornstarch
1 cup sugar
1 tablespoon grated lemon peel
Dash of nutmeg

¼ cup lemon juice
¼ cup butter or margarine
2 cups water
¼ teaspoon salt

Combine cornstarch, sugar and lemon peel. Add water slowly. Cook and stir until thick and clear. Remove from heat, add lemon juice, butter and nutmeg. Yields 3 cups.

LEMON SAUCE

1 cup boiling water
½ cup butter
1 cup sugar
½ to 1 teaspoon ground nutmeg

Juice of 1 lemon
1 lemon peel, grated
1 egg, beaten
2 tablespoons cornstarch

Boil water in medium saucepan. Add butter, sugar, nutmeg, lemon juice and rind. Cook over medium heat until butter melts. Remove from heat. Combine egg and cornstarch and stir until cornstarch is absorbed. Add to lemon mixture. Return to heat and cook until thick. Serve warm. Yields 2 cups. *Note:* You may use more lemon if you wish. *Delicious topping for a variety of desserts.*

Mary Suzanne Roehm
Grosse Pointe Woods, Michigan

MARSHMALLOW FUDGE SAUCE

1 large package miniature
  marshmallows

1 (12-ounce) package chocolate
  chips
1 (10-ounce) can evaporated milk

Put all ingredients in double boiler over medium heat and stir until thick and mixed well. Serve hot over ice cream or cake. Yields 1 quart.

Betsy Craig

MOCK HOLLANDIASE SAUCE

1 cup mayonnaise
1 teaspoon dry mustard

2 tablespoons horseradish
5 teaspoons lemon juice

In small bowl stir well the ingredients. Yields 1¼ cups.

K. C. Bennett

PEPPER JELLY

6½ cups sugar
1½ cups vinegar
1 bottle liquid fruit pectin

¾ cup green peppers
¼ cup hot (red) peppers

Puree peppers, ½ cup vinegar in blender. Mix sugar, vinegar with peppers, bring to rolling boil and boil 2 minutes. Remove from stove. Let stand 10 minutes. Skim, add liquid pectin and a few drops of food coloring. Yields 8 (4-ounce) jars.

K. C. Bennett

PESTO SAUCE

1 cup fresh basil
8 sprigs fresh parsley
½ cup pine nuts or walnuts
2 cloves garlic, crushed
⅓ cup Parmesan cheese

⅓ cup Romano cheese
¼ cup oil
2 tablespoons butter, softened
Salt to taste

Bring all ingredient together in blender or processor. Store in a covered container in refrigerator for several days. This is great on pasta, chicken and seafood. Yields 2½ to 3 cups.

PUMPKIN SHELL CASSEROLE

1 (10 or 12-inch) pumpkin or winter
   squash
4 apples, unpeeled and cubed
1 cup raisins
1 cup chopped nuts

2 oranges, peeled and chopped
½ cup maple syrup or honey
¼ teaspoon cinnamon
¼ teaspoon nutmeg

Scrub the pumpkin or squash, leaving the stem on for a handle. Carve out a 5 or 6-inch circle from the top and save for a cover. Dig out seeds and soft interior and discard. Mix apples, raisins, nuts, oranges, maple syrup (or honey), cinnamon and nutmeg. Spoon them into the shell. Put on the lid and place the filled shell in the oven on a pie plate. Bake at 400 degrees for 1 to 2 hours, until a fork can penetrate the shell. To serve, remove cover and serve on the table from the shell. Serves 6 to 8. *A healthy and fun to eat, attractive fall party or family dish.*

Lenore Marino, Jewel Box Emporium

SCALLOPED APPLES

6 large apples
¼ teaspoon salt
1 tablespoon lemon juice
¼ teaspoon cinnamon

¼ cup water
¾ cup sugar
¼ cup flour
⅓ cup butter

Pare, core and slice apples. Place in a buttered shallow baking dish. Pour salt, lemon juice, cinnamon and water over apples. Mix sugar, flour and butter until crumbly. Sprinkle on top of apple mixture. Bake at 400 degrees for 30 to 40 minutes. Serve with ham, pork, chicken or as brunch accompaniment. Serves 6.

SHOE PEG RELISH

1 can French-style seasoned green
   beans
1 can shoe peg corn
1 can baby English peas

1 green pepper, chopped
1 cup chopped celery
1 onion, chopped

Dressing
1 cup sugar
½ cup oil
¾ cup vinegar

1 teaspoon salt
1 teaspoon pepper

In container with a lid, mix together dressing ingredients. Heat ingredients and pour over vegetables. Keep covered and refrigerated up to a week. Serves 6 to 8. *Great picnic salad.*

Betty Deal
Medford, New Jersey

SPICY MAYONNAISE

¼ cup olive oil (good quality)
1 egg
3 medium cloves crushed garlic
1 teaspoon Dijon mustard
1 teaspoon salt

Few dashes cayenne pepper
1 cup safflower oil
3 tablespoons raw, unpasteurized,
   full strength apple cider
   vinegar

Combine first six ingredients in blender container and mix well on medium speed. Drizzle ½ cup oil very slowly into blender on low speed. Add vinegar, mix well. Add remaining oil, again very slowly at low speed. Yields approximately 1½ cups.

Jane Breazzano
Hawthorne, New Jersey

SPRING COMPOTE

4 navel oranges
1 pint fresh strawberries
½ cup of fruity white wine
1 tablespoon freshly grated ginger
  root

2 tablespoons chopped fresh
  coriander
Sugar to taste

Peel and slice oranges over a bowl to catch the juice. Place oranges and strawberries in the bowl. Add wine, ginger and coriander, mix gently. Let stand 1 hour. If strawberries are tart you may need the sugar. Chill. Serves 4 to 6. *This compote is served frequently in Paris in the spring. A favorite of the French.*

Ann S. Miller.

SUMMER'S BARBECUE SAUCE

1 quart chili sauce
2 tablespoons Worcestershire
  sauce
¼ cup apricot preserves

¼ cup soy sauce
½ cup brown sugar
Juice of 1 lemon

Cook in saucepan until sauce comes together. Brush on chicken, pork or beef or ribs and grill on the barbecue or bake in the oven. Yields 5 cups.

Maureen Horn, Summers

SWEET BELL PEPPER JAM

12 sweet red bell peppers
3 cups sugar

1 cup white vinegar
1 tablespoon salt

Grind peppers and let stand with salt for 30 minutes. Then add other ingredients with ¼ cup of the pepper juice. Bring to a boil and simmer until thick. Pour in glass jars and cover with paraffin. Yields about 2 to 2½ cups. *Excellent with cream cheese as hors d'oeuvres, or on toast for breakfast.*

Anita Laird

UNION LEAGUE SAUCE

1 small bottle catsup
¾ bottle chili sauce
¾ jar India relish

10 drops hot pepper sauce
1 tablespoon Worcestershire sauce

Mix all ingredients together. Yields 3 to 3½ cups. *Great on hamburgers.*

VANILLA EXTRACT

1 vanilla bean

1 pint brandy

Cut vanilla bean into several large pieces and add to pint of brandy. Close the cap and allow to set several weeks. Shake the bottle once every day. Yields 1 pint. *You will have a finer quality extract than is available commercially. You may even find you can use less than is called for in most recipes.*

Ada G. Tuttle

WINE WHIPPED CREAM

½ cup sifted powdered sugar
1 cup heavy cream, whipped

2 tablespoons California sweet or
cream sherry

Fold the sugar into the whipped cream. Then fold in the sherry. Yield 1 to 1½ cups. *Great dessert topper.*

Christy Igoe
Seaville, New Jersey

CHOCOLATE BUTTERNUT SAUCE

12 ounces milk or semi-sweet chocolate chips

1 cup butter
½ cup chopped pecans

Place chocolate chips and butter in top of double boiler. Cook over simmering water until melted and hot. (May also melt in heavy saucepan over very low heat). Stir in nuts just before serving. Serve warm over vanilla, coffee or peppermint ice cream. Sauce will harden on ice cream. Serves 8 to 10. *Keeps in refrigerator 1 month.*

Mary Suzanne Roehm
Grosse Pointe Woods, Michigan

Sweets

The Joseph Hall House, 1868
645 Hughes Street

Turn any corner in Cape May and you are sure to find well cared
for gardens, surrounded by wrought iron fences or picket
gates. This building is a fine example of such, along with a wonderful combination of color, embellishments, and intricate design. Tasteful thought has been given to every detail of this
lovely property.

GRASSHOPPER PIE

Chocolate cookie crust, homemade
or prepared
32 large marshmallows or 3 cups
miniatures
½ cup milk
¼ cup creme de menthe

3 tablespoons white creme de
cacao
1½ cups chilled whipping cream
Few drops green food coloring
(optional)

Heat marshmallows and milk over medium heat, stirring constantly, just until marshmallows are melted. Refrigerate until thickened. Stir in liqueurs. Beat whipping cream in chilled bowl until stiff. Add food coloring. Fold marshmallow mixture into whipped cream. Pour into crust. Sprinkle with grated semi-sweet chocolate. Refrigerate at least three hours. Serves 6.

Karen Andrus

MOCHA ANGEL PIE

3 egg whites
¼ teaspoon cream of tartar

¾ cup sugar

Heat oven to 275 degrees. Beat the egg whites with cream of tartar until frothy. Gradually beat in sugar until glossy smooth meringue is formed. Spread half of meringue in bottom and halfway up sides of very well buttered 9-inch pie plate (preferably glass). Drop mounds of remaining meringue along the rim of the plate or fill a pastry bag and pipe on. Bake for at least 1 hour or until slightly browned and crisp. Remove from oven and cool.

Filling
2 (12-ounce) packages semi-sweet
chocolate
¼ cup strong coffee (hot)

1 cup heavy whipped cream
1 teaspoon vanilla

During last twenty minutes of baking shell, put chocolate in oven to melt in oven-proof bowl. Remove and add hot coffee until blended and smooth. Add vanilla. Whip cream and blend into slightly cooled chocolate. Pour mixture into pie shell. Chill one hour. Serves 8. *I developed this pie for my sister who asked for a chocolate, low-cholesterol dessert.*

Diane Muentz, Alexander's Inn

QUEEN VICTORIA'S CORONATION TART

1 envelope unflavored gelatin
¼ cup cold water
4 eggs yolks, beaten
⅓ cup sugar
1 tablespoon grated lemon rind
½ cup lemon juice
1 baked 9-inch rich pastry shell

1 tablespoon lemon juice
1 tablespoon cornstarch
½ cup maraschino cherry juice
1½ cups drained maraschino
  cherries
1 cup heavy cream, whipped

Soften the gelatin in the cold water. Blend the egg yolks, sugar, lemon rind and ⅓ cup lemon juice together, in top of double boiler, cook over boiling water for about 8 minutes, stirring constantly until thickened. Add the gelatin and cook, stirring constantly for about 3 minutes or until gelatin is dissolved. Cool until slightly thickened then fold in the whipped cream. Turn into the pastry shell and chill until set. Blend the cornstarch with the cherry juice and cook over low heat, stirring constantly until thickened. Stir in 1 tablespoon lemon juice and the cherries. Top cooled tart with the cherry mixture. Chill. Serves 8 to 12. *Top with wine whipped cream or sweet whipped cream.*

Christy Igoe
Seaville, New Jersey

LEMON FLUFF PIE

1 baked 9-inch pie shell
4 eggs
¼ cup lemon juice

1 cup sugar
Grated rind of 1 lemon
3 tablespoons water

Separate the eggs, putting the whites in a mixing bowl, the yolks in top of double boiler. Beat yolks until thick, add the lemon juice and rind, the water and ½ the sugar. Cook over hot water, stirring until thick. Remove from hot water. Beat whites until fluffy, add remaining sugar and continue beating into a fine, soft meringue. Fold half the meringue into the warm egg/lemon mixture. When evenly blended heap into baked pie shell. Make wreath around the edge of pie with remaining meringue and set in 425 degree oven about 10 minutes or long enough to brown meringue lightly. Serves. 6 to 8. *This pie is pleasantly tart and has never failed to turn out well for me. I usually use a pre-baked graham cracker crust pie shell.*

Jessie C. Daniels
Arlington, Virginia

TOM'S RUM CREAM PIE

1 (6-ounce) box zwieback crackers
1 cup plus 2 tablespoons sugar
½ teaspoon cinamon
½ cup soft butter
6 egg yolks

1 envelope unflavored gelatin
½ cup water
1 pint cream
½ cup dark rum

To make pie shell, crush crackers and mix with 2 tablespoons sugar, cinnamon and butter. Press mixture into a 10-inch pie plate. Set aside. Blend 6 eggs until light and creamy. Add 1 cup sugar. Soak gelatin in cold water then bring to a boil over low heat. Pour over sugar and egg mixture stirring briskly. Whip 1 pint cream until stiff. Fold into egg mixture, add rum. Cool until mixture sets. Pour into shell and chill in refrigerator until firm. Serves 6 to 8. *If desired shave semi-sweet chocolate over top.*

Tom Williams

SHOO-FLY PIE

3 cups flour
1 cup light brown sugar
½ cup shortening
Pinch of salt
2 cups light brown sugar

2 eggs
1 cup old fashioned syrup
2 cups water
1 teaspoon baking soda
2 (9-inch) unbaked pie crusts

Combine first 4 (four) ingredients to make crumbs, set aside. Mix 2 cups brown sugar and eggs, then syrup, water and baking soda. Pour liquid into unbaked pie crusts and top with crumbs. Bake at 350 degrees for 50 to 55 minutes. Serves 12 to 16. *This is a traditional Pennsylvania Dutch Shoo-Fly pie. It also appears on Mrs. Schlorer's jar of Golden table syrup. Any type of molasses or light table syrup may be used.*

Phyllis M. Stauffer
Boyertown, Pennsylvania

WHOLE STRAWBERRY PIE

1 cup sugar
3½ teaspoons cornstarch
⅓ cup cold water
2 quarts strawberries

Juice of ½ lemon
1 cup heavy cream, whipped
1 (9-inch) pastry shell, baked

Mix sugar, cornstarch and cold water. Add to ½ quart berries. Heat on stove until it comes to a boil or thickens. Remove from stove and add lemon juice. Combine with remaining berries and pile into shell. Spread top with whipped cream. Serves 6 to 8.

Ruth Lindsay

PECAN CHEESE PIE

1 (8-ounce) package cream cheese
⅓ cup sugar
¼ teaspoon salt
1 teaspoon vanilla
1 egg
1 (10-inch) pastry shell, unbaked

1¼ to 1½ cups chopped pecans
3 eggs
¼ cup granulated sugar
1 cup dark corn syrup
1 teaspoon vanilla

Mix first 5 ingredients well and place in unbaked 10-inch pie shell. Sprinkle pecans over cheese mixture. Mix until blended: 3 eggs, sugar, corn syrup and vanillla. Place on top of pecans. Bake in 10-inch pie shell at 350 degrees for 35 to 40 minutes. Serves 8. *(Pie will split when baking)*.

Loretta Baver
Pennsburg, Pennsylvania

APPLE CANDY PIE

6 cups apples peeled, cored and
  sliced
¾ cup sugar
4 tablespoons flour
1 (9-inch) pie shell
2 tablespoons butter

2 tablespoons lemon juice
4 tablespoons butter
½ cup brown sugar
2 tablespoons milk
½ cup pecans

Combine apples, ¾ cup sugar, and flour. Place in pie shell, dot with 2 tablespoons butter and sprinkle 2 tablespoons lemon juice over the top. Bake in at 400 degrees for 50 minutes. While pie is baking, melt 4 tablespoons butter. Stir in ½ cup brown sugar and 2 tablespoons milk, heat to boiling. Remove form heat and add ½ cup peacns. Spread over top of pie when done, return to oven for 5 minutes, until topping bubbles and crust is glazed. Cool at least 1 hour before cutting. Serves 6 to 8. *Can be messy but it is a terrific tasting dessert.*

Doralene Davis
Ardmore, Pennsylvania

APPLE CRUMB PIE

4 large tart apples
1 unbaked pie shell
1 cup sugar

1 teaspoon cinnamon
¾ cup flour
⅓ cup butter or margarine

Peel the apples and cut into eighths, then arrange in the pie shell. Mix ½ cup sugar with the cinnamon and sprinkle over the apples. Sift the remaining sugar with the flour then cut in the butter until crumbly. Sprinkle over the apples. Bake at 400 degrees for 40 to 50 minutes. Serve warm or cool. Serves 6 to 8.

Sandy Miller, The Windward House

APRICOT DELIGHT PIE

2 cups (17-ounce can) apricot
halves and syrup
1 (3½-ounce) package vanilla
pudding and pie filling
1½ cups evaporated milk

1 egg yolk, beaten
9-inch pie shell, baked
2 teaspoons cornstarch
¼ cup toasted, sliced almonds

Drain apricots, reserving syrup. Place pudding mix in a medium saucepan and gradually stir in evaporated milk, ½ cup syrup and beaten egg yolk. Cook over medium heat stirring frequently until mixture boils. Chop ½ cup apricots and stir into pudding. Pour into pie shell and chill 1 hour. In another medium saucepan, add ⅔ cup syrup (add water if needed) and cornstarch. Cook over medium heat, stirring frequently until mixture boils for 1 minute. Cut remaining apricots lengthwise into thirds. Arrange slices over pudding layer and spoon glaze over pie filling. Place almonds around the pie's edge. Chill until ready to serve. Serves 8 to 10.

Mason Cottage

BANANA-CARAMEL PIE

1 (14-ounce) can sweetened
condensed milk
2 to 3 bananas, average size
1 (9-inch) graham cracker crust

1 cup whipping cream
¼ cup powdered sugar
1 to 2 English toffee-flavored
candy bars, crumbled

Pour milk into an 8-inch glass pie plate. Cover with foil. Pour about ¼ inch hot water in a larger shallow pan. Place pie plate in larger pan. Bake at 425 degrees for 1 hour 20 minutes or until milk is thick and caramel colored. (Keep adding hot water to largar pan to keep water at ¼ inch.) Remove foil and set aside. Cut bananas crosswise into ⅛ inch slices; place in graham cracker crust. Spread caramelized milk over banana layer. Cool. Combine whipping cream and powdered sugar, beat until stiff. Spread over caramel layer. Sprinkle with crumbled candy. Chill several hours. Serves 8.

Christy Lgoe
Seaville, New Jersey

BANANA SPLIT SUNDAE PIE

1 quart strawberry ice cream,
  softened
1 graham cracker pie crust
2 ripe bananas

1 to 1½ cups whipped cream
Chopped pecans
Cherries

Spoon ½ of the ice cream into graham cracker crust. Smooth top. Split bananas lengthwise and in half. Arrange bananas, spoke style, on the ice cream. Layer the remaining ice cream over bananas. Swirl top. Freeze until firm (about 2 hours). Decorate with whipped cream, pecans and cherries. Serves 8. *This is a recipe that is quick, easy, delicious, but tastes like it took a long time to prepare. It's good for a dessert in a hurry.*

Kristie Walz
Leonia, New Jersey

BLACK WALNUT PIE

1 (9-inch) pastry crust, unbaked
3 eggs
1 cups dark corn syrup
⅔ cup dark brown sugar

⅛ teaspoon salt (optional)
⅓ cup butter or margarine,
  melted
1 cup black walnut pieces

Prepare pie crust in your usual way. Line 9-inch pie plate. Beat together eggs, syrup, brown sugar, salt and melted butter. Add black walnuts. Beat some more. Pour into unbaked pie shell. Bake at 350 degrees for 50 minutes. Cool. Serves 6 to 8. *Good with a dab of vanilla ice cream. But (1) what isn't? (2)totally unnecessary.*

Bob Cunningham

CHOCOLATE BANANA CREME PIE

¾ cup small semi-sweet chocolate
  bits, divided
3 cups frozen non-dairy whipped
  topping with real cream,
  divided

2 eggs
1 (9-inch) pie shell, baked
2 medium bananas

Heat oven to 350 degrees. In saucepan, melt ½ cup chocolate chips over low heat. Remove from heat and stir in 1 cup whipped topping. Beat eggs and add to mixture. Pour into baked pie shell and bake for 30 minutes. Cool 10 minutes. Slice 1½ bananas and layer on pie. Top with 2 cups whipped topping. Chill 1 hour. Top with remaining chocolate chips and banana slices. Serves 8 to 10.

Joan Mason

COCONUT PIE CRUST

1½ cups flaked coconut
2 tablespoons melted butter or
  margarine

¼ cup graham cracker crumbs
2 tablespoons sugar
1 (8-inch) pie pan

Mix coconut and butter or margarine. Add graham cracker crumbs and sugar. Mix. Press into a greased pie pan to form shell. Bake at 375 degrees for 10 to 12 minutes. Cool. Yields 1 crust. *Delicious filled with ice cream.*

K.C. Bennett

MUD PIE

Chocolate pie crust
3 tablespoons butter, melted
1 quart coffee ice cream, softened

1 (8-ounce) jar hot fudge topping
1 cup whipped cream
3 ounces almonds, slivered

Brush pie crust with butter. Bake 325 degrees for 7 minutes. Let cool. Fill crust with coffee ice cream. Put in freezer until hard. Top with cold hot fudge topping. Put in freezer again until hard. When ready to serve, top with whipped cream and almonds. Serves 8. *Very rich and sinfully delicious.*

Katie Gregg

FRENCH SILK PIE

¾ cup butter (not margarine)
1¼ cups sugar
2½ squares bitter chocolate, melted
1½ teaspoons vanilla

3 eggs
1 cup heavy cream whipped
1 (9-inch) cooked pie crust
Semi-sweet chocolate bits for garnish

Beat butter until fluffy. Add sugar and continue beating until creamed. Add chocolate and vanilla, beat again. Add eggs one at a time, beating 3 minutes after each egg is added. Taste to be sure there in no grainy feeling (sugar is all dissolved). Spoon into pie crust. Chill. Top with whipped cream and chocolate chips. Chill until served. Serves 8.

Linda Amos

FUDGE PIE

1 cup butter
2 cups sugar
4 egg yolks
4 squares semi-sweet chocolate, melted

¾ cup bread flour
2 teaspoons vanilla
4 egg whites
¼ teaspoon salt

Beat butter until soft, then add sugar gradually, blending until creamy. Beat in 4 egg yolks. Beat in the melted chocolate. Beat in the flour and vanilla. Whip egg whites and salt until stiff, then fold into batter. Bake in greased 8½-inch glass pie plate at 325 degrees for about 30 minutes. Serves 8 to 12. *Serve topped with ice cream of whipped cream, or just serve without topping to save some calories!*

Donna Gaver Shank
Dover, Delaware

ICE CREAM PIE

1½ cups flaked coconut
2 tablespoons melted butter
¼ cup graham cracker crumbs

2 tablespoons sugar
Your choice of ice cream, softened

Mix coconut with melted butter. Add graham cracker crumbs and sugar. Press into greased pie pan to form crust. Bake at 375 degrees for 10 to 12 minutes. When cool, fill with your favorite ice cream. Freeze until ready to use. Serves 6 to 8.

Sue Leaming

LEMON CREAM PIE

1 cup sugar
2 tablespoons butter
2 tablespoons flour
2 eggs

1 cup milk
Juice of 1 lemon
Grated rind of 1 lemon
1 pie shell, partially baked

Cream sugar and butter together. Add flour, stirring until mixed. Separate eggs and add egg yolks. Beat this mixture until smooth, then add milk, lemon juice and rind. Fold in egg whties, beaten stiff, and pour into partially baked crust. Bake at 425 degrees for 10 minutes, then lower oven temperature to 325 degrees. Bake until filling is firm to touch. Serves 6. *A family recipe from a loving mother-in-law, Katie Robbins, ever an aid and comfort to an inexperienced young cook.*

Mrs. Lib Robbins

MANDARIN ORANGE PIE

1 (4-ounce) can mandarin oranges
1 (9-inch) pie shell, baked
2 to 3 firm bananas
1 package instant banana pudding
   mix

¾ cup milk
½ pint whipping cream
½ teaspoon vanilla
1 small can flaked coconut

Drain the oranges and arrange in pie shell. Slice the bananas over orange slices. Combine pudding mix, milk, whipping cream and vanilla and beat with mixer until slightly thickened. Pour over sliced fruit and sprinkle with coconut. Refrigerate for 1 hour or longer before serving. Serves 6 to 8. *Good to make the night before, or the morning of.*

FLAKY PIE CRUST

3 cups flour
1¼ cups vegetable shortening
5 tablespoons cold water

1 egg
1 tablespoon vinegar
Salt to taste

Combine. Roll out between 2 pieces of plastic wrap. Yields 2 (9-inch) pie crusts.

Joan Alvarez

MANDARIN ORANGE PINEAPPLE CAKE

1 box golden butter cake mix
1 (11-ounce) can mandarin oranges
  with juice

4 eggs
½ cup oil

Icing
1 (21-ounce) can crushed pineapple
1 container prepared whipped
  topping

1 box instant vanilla pudding

Mix first 4 ingredients at low speed until moistened, then at medium speed for 2 minutes. Pour into 3 (8-inch) or 2 (9-inch) cake pans, greased and floured. Bake at 325 degrees for 30 minutes. Remove from oven and cool. Mix icing ingredients. Remove cooled cake from pans and ice. Store cake in refrigerator until ready to serve.

Gurd Tolley

JEWISH APPLE CAKE

2 teaspoons sugar
2 teaspoons cinnamon
4 eggs
2 cups sugar
1 cup oil
3 cups sifted flour

3 teaspoons baking powder
½ teaspoon salt
½ cup orange juice
1 tablespoon vanilla
½ cup raisins (optional)
4 or 5 large apples

Preheat oven to 350 degrees, grease and flour 10-inch tube pan. Pare and slice apples and set aside. Combine 2 teaspoons sugar with 2 teaspoons cinnamon and set aside. In large bowl beat eggs and add sugar gradually. Then beat in oil. Sift together flour, baking powder and salt. Add flour mixture and orange juice alternately to eggs and sugar. Add vanilla. Pour ¼ batter into pan, arrange ⅓ of the sliced apples on top, sprinkle with ⅓ cinnamon and sugar mixture. Repeat, ending with batter. Bake at 350 degrees for 1½ hours. Cool. Serves 8 to 10. *Great with tea or coffee. Can be frozen.*

Ruth Kurland

HAWAIIAN WEDDING CAKE

1 yellow cake mix
1 (20-ounce) can crushed pineapple
1 (8-ounce) package cream cheese
1 (3⅜-ounce) box instant vanilla
   pudding

2 cups milk
1 (16-ounce) container frozen
   non-dairy whipped topping
Coconut

Grease and flour 13x9x2-inch pan. Prepare the yellow cake mix as directed on box. Pour into prepared pan and bake as directed. Cool cake. Pour the crushed pineapple over cake, juice and all. Set aside. Prepare in blender cream cheese, pudding and milk. Pour over pineapple. Top with container of whipped topping. Sprinkle with coconut. Refrigerate. Serves 12 to 15.

Judy Nuss

HONEY TWIST COFFEE CAKE

3 to 3¼ cups unbleached flour
¼ cup sugar
1 teaspoon salt
1 package active dry yeast

1 cup milk
3 tablespoons butter or margarine
2 eggs (reserve 1 white)

In large bowl combine 1½ cups flour, sugar, salt and yeast. Heat milk and butter until thermometer registers 120 to 130 degrees (butter does not need to melt). Add heated liquid and egg, less one white, to flour mixture. Blend on low speed until moistened. Beat 3 minutes medium speed. Stir in remaining 1½ to 1¾ cups flour to form a soft dough. Knead until smooth, approximately 1 minute. Place in greased bowl. Cover. Let rise until doubled in size, 30 to 40 minutes. Generously grease 12 cup fluted tube pan. Punch down dough. On floured surface, shape dough into long roll about 1-inch in diameter. Twist roll into prepared pan, beginning at inner edge and coiling out.

Topping
¼ cup butter or soft margarine
2 tablespoons honey

⅔ cup powdered sugar
Reserved egg white

Combine topping ingredients. Brush ½ of topping over dough. Let rise until doubled in size. Bake at 350 degrees for 30 to 45 minutes until golden brown. Remove from pan immediately. Brush warm cake with remaining topping. Serve warm or cool. Serves 12. *Recipe is from a 1977 Pillsbury recipe book. My niece convinced me that using yeast was easy (it just takes time) and gave me this recipe. It has always worked well.*

Fran Prichard, Duke of Windsor Inn

FUNNY CAKE

2 cups sugar
½ cup shortening
2 eggs
1 cup milk
2 cups flour

2 teaspoons baking powder
½ cup cocoa
1 cup sugar
1 cup hot water
2 pie shells, unbaked

Mix first 6 ingredients well and set aside. Mix cocoa, sugar and hot water. Set aside. Place first mixture in unbaked pie shells and pour cocoa mixture over top. Bake at 350 degrees for 1 hour. Cool. Serves 6. *This is a Pennsylvania Dutch breakfast cake.*

Mrs. Gordon Baver
Pennsburg, Pennsylvania

FUDGE PUDDING CAKE

1 cup flour
2 teaspoons baking powder
1 teaspoon salt
⅔ cup sugar
2 tablespoons cocoa
½ cup milk

1 teaspoon vanilla
2 tablespoons melted butter
½ cup chopped nuts
1 cup brown sugar
¼ cup cocoa
½ cup boiling water

Sift together 3 times, flour, baking powder, salt, sugar and 2 tablespoons cocoa. Set aside. Combine milk, vanilla, melted butter, and add to flour mixture. Beat until smooth. Stir in ½ cup chopped nuts. Grease a 6-cup casserole and spread mixture into it. In another bowl mix brown sugar and ¼ cup cocoa. Sprinkle over the batter. Pour boiling water over entire cake. Bake at 350 degrees for 50 minutes. Cool. Serves 6.

Linda Reeves
Neptune Beach, Florida

MINCEMEAT BRUNCH CAKE

1½ cups sugar
1 cup butter or margarine,
  softened
1½ teaspoons baking powder
1½ teaspoons vanilla
½ teaspoon grated orange peel

4 eggs
3 cups flour
2 cups mincemeat
⅔ cup chopped walnuts
1 cup powdered sugar
2 tablespoons orange juice

Beat together sugar and butter until creamy. Beat in baking powder, vanilla and orange peel. Add eggs, one at a time, beating well after each addition. Mix in flour. Spread ⅔ batter in a greased 15x10-inch jelly roll pan. Spread mincemeat on top of batter. Drop remaining batter onto mincemeat, making 15 dollops. Sprinkle chopped nuts over all. Bake in a 350 degree oven for 35 to 40 minutes, or until tester inserted in center comes out clean. Stir together powdered sugar and orange juice and drizzle over cake while still warm. Cut in squares and serve warm. Serves 15. *A Thanksgiving and Christmas morning breakfast tradition at The Queen Victoria. This recipe was featured in November/December 1985 issue of Americana.*

Joan Wells, The Queen Victoria

CHESS CAKE

1 box yellow cake mix
1 box powdered sugar
½ cup butter, softened

3 eggs
1 (8-ounce) package cream cheese

Combine cake mix, butter and 1 egg, mix well. Pat down into 13x9-inch greased pan. Cream the cheese with 2 eggs and powdered sugar. Pour over the top of cake mixture. Bake at 350 degrees 40 to 45 minutes or until golden brown on top. Let cool 4 hours. Cake settles when cool. Cut in desired pieces, like bars. Serves 24.

Mary Suzanne Roehm
Grosse Pointe Woods, Michigan

CRANBERRY CAKE

½ cup butter or shortening
1½ cups sugar
2 eggs
1 teaspoon red food coloring
1 cup buttermilk
2½ cups sifted flour
1 teaspoon baking soda

1 teaspoon salt
3 tablespoons cocoa
1 teaspoon vinegar
1½ cups cranberries
¼ cup chopped walnuts
¼ cup water
1 orange rind, grated

Grease and flour two 8-inch cake pans. Cook cranberries with walnuts in water until skins pop and berries are soft. Cool. Cream the butter and sugar, add eggs, food coloring and orange rind. Sift together flour, baking soda, salt and cocoa. Add vinegar to buttermilk. Mix sifted ingredients alternately with buttermilk into the egg mixture. Fold in cranberries. Bake at 325 degrees 25 to 30 minutes. Cool and frost. Serves 10 to 12.

Maureen Horn

CRANBERRY CAKE FROSTING

1 cup milk
1 cup sugar
½ cup butter

½ cup cream cheese
5 tablespoons flour
1 teaspoon vanilla

Mix flour and sugar in a saucepan. Whisk in milk and cook until thickened. Cool. Cream butter and cream cheese until smooth. Beat in flour mixture and vanilla. Chill. Beat occasionally until thick enough to spread. Frost cake. Yields enough frosting to frost 1 (13x9-inch) cake.

Maureen Horn

COCONUT CARROT CAKE

2 cups flour
2½ teaspoons baking soda
2 teaspoons cinnamon
1 teaspoon salt
1 cup oil
2 cups sugar

3 eggs
1 (8-ounce) can crushed pineapple
  in juice
2 cups grated carrots
1½ cups coconut
½ cup chopped nuts

Mix flour, baking soda, cinnamon and salt. Beat oil, sugar and eggs thoroughly. Add flour mixture and beat on medium until smooth. Add pineapple, carrots, coconut and nuts. Pour into a greased 13x9-inch pan. Bake at 350 degrees for 50 to 60 minutes. Cool on rack 10 minutes. Remove from pan and finish cooling. Frost with coconut cream frosting. Serves 12 to 16.

Blanche Rogers
Jax Beach, Florida

COCONUT CREAM FROSTING

1 (3-ounce) package cream cheese
¼ cup butter
3 cups powdered sugar

1 tablespoon milk
½ teaspoon vanilla
1 cup coconut, toasted

Cream the cream cheese with the butter. Alternately add the powdered sugar, milk and vanilla. Beat until smooth. Add ½ cup coconut and frost cake. Sprinkle ½ cup coconut on top of cake. Yields frosting for 1 (13x9-inch) cake or 2 (8 or 9-inch) layers.

Blanche Rogers
Jax Beach, Florida

COFFEE CAKE

1 box brown sugar
2 eggs
1 cup brewed coffee
1 cup oil
3 cups flour
1 teaspoon vanilla

1 teaspoon salt
1 teaspoon baking soda
1 (6-ounce) package semi-sweet
   chocolate bits
½ cup chopped nuts

Grease 13x9-inch pan. Mix first 8 ingredients together. Top with chocolate bits and nuts. Bake at 375 degrees for 30 to 35 minutes. Serves 6 to 8. *Easy, good, fast breakfast.*

Doris Williams

EASY CHEESE CAKE

1 cup sugar
2 teaspoons vanilla

3 (8-ounce) cream cheese at room
temperature
4 eggs

Mix all together. Beat until smooth. Pour into 9x9-inch glass dish or buttered tin plate. Bake at 350 degrees for 30 minutes. Serves 6 to 8. Easy -easy-easy.

Joan Warner

1-2-3-4-CAKE

1 cup margarine
2 cups sugar
4 eggs
3 cups flour

3 teaspoons baking powder
1 teaspoon salt
1 cup milk
2 teaspoons vanilla

Grease and flour 12 cup tube pan. Mix ingredients in order given until smooth. Bake at 375 degrees for 1 hour. Cool and remove from pan. Dust with powdered sugar or dribble with icing. Serves 12.

Clair Menge

DUNDEE (WHITE FRUIT) CAKE

2 cups sugar
1½ cups butter
3 eggs
1 cup milk
4 cups flour
2 teaspoons baking powder
½ teaspoon salt
½ cup chopped nuts
1½ cups white raisins
1 pound fruit mix
1 tablespoon grated lemon rind
1 tablespoon flour

Cream sugar and butter, add eggs, then milk. Sift together flour, baking powder and salt. Add to butter mixture stirring until smooth. Mix nuts, raisins and fruit, coat with 1 tablespoon flour. Add lemon rind and stir into batter thoroughly. Pour into greased and floured 12 cup tube pan, bundt pan, small individual loaf pans or cupcake pans. Bake at 350 degrees for 1 to 1½ hours. Cool and remove from pans. Serves 12 to 20. *Nice for gift at Christmas with glaze frosting decorated with candied fruit.*

Eileen M. Bastek

BETTER THAN–CAKE

1 yellow cake mix with pudding
1 (20-ounce) can crushed pineapple
1 cup sugar
1 teaspoon cornstarch
1 (6-ounce) box instant vanilla
  pudding
3 bananas, sliced
1 large container frozen non-dairy
  whipped topping
1 cup chopped nuts
1 cup shredded coconut

Grease and flour 13x9-inch pan. Preheat oven to 350 degrees. Mix the cake mix and bake according to package directions. Cool. In saucepan, combine pineapple, sugar and cornstarch. Cook over medium heat 6 to 10 minutes until slightly thickened. Spread over cooled cake. Mix instant pudding according to directions, let thicken. Slice 3 bananas and arrange on top of the pineapple, then spread the thickened pudding over the bananas. Top with non-dairy topping and sprinkle with nuts and coconut. Chill well before serving. Serves 12. *Must be made ahead to allow chilling time.*

Lynda Leaming
Orange, California

CARROT, RAISIN, PRUNE CAKE
An Easy Food Processor Recipe

2 cups flour	¾ cup pecans
2 teaspoons baking soda	5 carrots, scrubbed and trimmed
2 teaspoons baking powder	4 large eggs
1 teaspoon salt	2 cups sugar
¼ teaspoon nutmeg	½ cup oil
¼ teaspoon ground allspice	¾ cup golden raisins
1 tablespoon cinnamon	2 tablespoons powdered sugar
7 large dried pitted prunes	

Metal blade: Put flour, baking soda, baking powder, salt and spices in work bowl and process for 2 seconds. Leave about 1 tablespoon mixture in bowl, remove remaining and reserve it. Put prunes in work bowl and process for 10 seconds to chop them. Add nuts and process for 5 seconds. Transfer this mixture to a large bowl. Shredding Disc: Shred carrots (about 3 cups of shredded carrots). Add to prune mixture and combine with spoon. Metal Blade: Put eggs and sugar in work bowl, process for 1 minute or until light colored and thick. With machine running pour oil through feed tube and process for 1 minute. Stop machine once to scrape sides. Add prune, carrot mixture, raisins, process for 3 seconds. Add dry ingredients and combine by turning machine on and off 5 or 6 times or until flour disappears. Do not over process. Pour batter into a 12 cup greased and floured bundt pan. Bake at 325 degrees for 55 minutes. Cool and remove from pan. Sift powdered sugar on top. Serves 18 pieces. *An easy food processor cake for breakfast.*

Joan Echevarria-Gingerbread House

AUNT OLGA'S POUND CAKE

3 cups flour
1 tablespoon baking powder
Pinch of salt
1 cup butter
½ cup shortening

3 cups sugar
6 eggs
1 cup milk
2 tablespoons vanilla

Sift together dry ingredients. Cream together butter, shortening, sugar and eggs. Add dry ingredients alternately with milk and vanilla (mixed). Bake in greased and floured tube pan at 350 degrees for 50 minutes or longer until cake tester comes out clean. Cool. Dust top with powdered sugar or frost. Serves 10 to 12. *Cake stays fresh for quite a few days. The recipe was given to me by "Aunt Olga" (thus the name) and is a family favorite.*

M. Edna Andrus
Haddon Township, New Jersey

VICTORIAN CURRANT CAKES
From Original Mac Cookbook

1 cup currants
½ cup brandy, heated
1 cup unsalted butter
1 heaping cup sugar
1 egg white

1 egg yolk
½ teaspoon nutmeg
½ teaspoon cinnamon
2½ to 2¾ cups flour

Soak currants in brandy for 30 minutes. Drain and reserve brandy. Cream butter with sugar until light. Add egg white, yolk and spices and mix well. Gradually add flour to make a smooth dough. Wrap in waxed paper and chill 1 hour. Pinch off small pieces of dough and roll with floured hands into 1-inch balls. Put on buttered cookie sheet, 2-inches apart and flatten with fork. Bake at 350 degrees for 10 minutes or until pale golden brown. Yields 4½ to 5 dozen.

BLUEBERRY BRUNCH CAKE

1 cup flour
1½ teaspoons baking powder
1 teaspoon salt
¾ cup sugar

¼ cup shortening
1 egg
½ cup milk
2 cups floured blueberries

Sift together flour, baking powder and salt in bowl. Set aside. Mix sugar and shortening. Add egg and mix. Beginning and ending with flour mixture, add flour mixture and milk alternately to sugar mixture. Fold in blueberries and pour batter into 9-inch square cake pan.

Topping
½ cup sugar or light brownulated
⅓ cup flour

1 teaspoon cinnamon
¼ cup butter, softened

Blend all ingredients together, using cold butter to prevent it from becoming pasty. Sprinkle on top of batter and bake at 350 degrees for 45 minutes. Serves 8 to 12. *May substitute raspberries when in season. An easy, do ahead recipe.*

The Mason Cottage

APPLE CAKE

1½ cup oil
2 cups sugar
3 eggs
2 teaspoons vanilla
3 cups flour

1 teaspoon soda
1 teaspoon salt
3 cups diced raw apples
1 cup chopped pecans
1 cup raisins

Blend oil and sugar well. Add eggs and vanilla. Sift flour, soda, salt together, keeping ½ cup to flour fruit and nuts. Add flour to mixture, then add floured fruit and nuts. Mix well. Pour into greased and floured tube pan. Bake at 350 degrees for 1 hour and 30 minutes. Serves 10 to 12.

Glaze
1 tablespoon vanilla
½ cup buttermilk
½ teaspoon soda

1 stick butter
1 cup sugar

Boil 5 minutes, stirring constantly. Spoon over hot cake. Let stand in pan overnight.

BANANA CREAM COFFEE CAKE

1 (8-ounce) package cream cheese,
  softened
⅓ cup sugar
1 tablespoon flour
½ teaspoon nutmeg
1 egg
½ cup butter, softened
1½ cups sugar
2 eggs
1 teaspoon baking soda

3 tablespoons hot water
3 cups flour
1 teaspoon baking powder
½ teaspoon salt
½ teaspoon nutmeg
½ teaspoon cinnamon
⅓ cup orange juice
1 teaspoon vanilla
3 bananas, mashed
1 cup chopped pecans

Combine first four ingredients, beating until smooth. Add one egg, and mix well. Set aside. Cream ½ cup butter. Gradually add 1½ cups sugar beating well. Add two eggs, one at a time, beating after each addition. Combine soda and water and add to creamed mixture. Combine flour, baking powder, salt, nutmeg, and cinnamon. Add to creamed mixture alternately with juice. Stir in vanilla, bananas, and pecans. Spoon 1½ cups banana mixture into a greased and floured bundt pan. Spread cream cheese mixture over batter. Spoon remaining batter over cream cheese mixture. Bake at 350 degrees for 50 to 55 minutes. Serves 10 to 12.

GRACE GILMAN'S GINGERBREAD
From Original Mac Cookbook

1 cup molasses
1 teaspoon salt
1 teaspoon ginger
1 teaspoon lard or drippings

¼ cup hot water
1 teaspoon baking soda
2 cups flour

Put molasses, salt, ginger, and lard into a bowl. Stir well, add hot water and soda stiffened with flour. Beat until smooth. Bake in a well-greased shallow pan in a moderately hot 350 degree oven for 20 to 30 minutes. Serves 10 to 12.

RUM CAKE

1 golden yellow cake mix
4 eggs
1 package vanilla instant pudding
½ cup oil

½ cup water
½ cup light rum
Pecans to cover bottom of bundt pan

Mix and beat all ingredients except pecans. Grease and flour bundt pan, cover bottom with pecans. Pour mix over pecans. Bake at 350 degrees for 45 to 60 minutes. Serves 10 to 12.

Glaze
½ cup butter
1 cup sugar

¼ to ½ cup rum

Combine ingredients in saucepan. Bring to a boil and cook 1 minute. As soon as cake comes from oven, pour glaze over. Let stand 30 minutes before removing from pan. Serves 10.

Elizabeth Toner

BUTTER CRUMB BREAKFAST CAKE

3 cups flour
Pinch of salt
2 cups sugar
4 tablespoons butter

3 teaspoons baking powder
2 eggs
1¼ cups milk

Mix first four ingredients well. Set 2 ounces aside. Add remaining ingredients. Mix well and pour into three 8-inch pie dishes. Sprinkle remaining crumbs over batter. Bake at 350 degrees for 30 minutes or until golden brown. Serves 6 to 8. *This was always my children's favorite.*

Loretta Baver
Pennsburg, Pennsylvania

CREME DE MENTHE CAKE SQUARES

1 cup sugar
½ cup butter
4 eggs, beaten
1 (16-ounce) can chocolate syrup

1 cup flour
½ teaspoon salt
1 teaspoon vanilla

Mix ingredients together. Place in a greased and floured 13x9-inch pan. Bake at 350 degrees for 40 to 50 minutes.

First Layer
2 cups powdered sugar
3 teaspoons green creme de
   menthe

½ cup butter, softened

While cake is cooling, mix ingredients. Spread over cooled cake.

Second Layer
6 ounces semi-sweet chocolate
   bits

6 tablespoons butter

Melt chocolate chips and butter. Cool slightly and spread over mint layer. Chill 5 to 10 minutes and cut into squares. Serves 10 to 15.

Joan Echevarria

PRUNE CAKE

1 teaspoon baking soda
1 cup sour milk
1½ cups sugar
½ cup shortening
2 eggs

2 cups flour
1 teaspoon baking powder
½ teaspoon cloves
½ teaspoon cinnamon
1 cup chopped cooked prunes

Mix baking soda in milk. Add ingredients in the order given, beating well after each addition. Bake in a slow 325 degree oven for about 35 minutes, or until done. Cool and remove from pan. Dust with powdered sugar if desired. Serves 12. *Very nice moist cake.*

Anna O. Hopkins
Adamstown, Pennsylvania

WALNUT RUM CAKE

1 cup black walnut bits
½ cup seedless raisins
1 package yellow cake mix (2 layer)
1 (3¾-ounce) package vanilla pudding

½ cup oil
½ cup dark rum
½ cup cold water
4 eggs
2 tablespoons creamy peanut butter

Sprinkle nuts and raisins in bottom of greased and floured 10-inch tube pan. In mixing bowl combine cake mix, pudding, oil, rum, and cold water. Beat at medium speed to blend well. Add eggs one at a time, add peanut butter. Beat 2 minutes at top speed. Pour into tube pan. Bake at 350 degrees 1 hour or until tests done. Cool, remove from pan. Serves 14. *Works best with pudding added to mix rather than included in mix. May be habit forming if eaten regularly for one week or more!*

Bob Cunningham

CREME DE MENTHE SQUARES

1¼ cups margarine, divided
½ cup unsweetened cocoa powder
3½ cups sifted powder sugar, divided
1 egg beaten

1 teaspoon vanilla
2 cups graham cracker crumbs
⅓ cup green creme de menthe
1½ cups semi-sweet chocolate bits

Bottom layer: in saucepan heat and stir ½ cup margarine and cocoa until well blended. Remove from heat, add ½ cup powdered sugar, beaten egg, vanilla and graham cracker crumbs. Mix well and press into bottom of ungreased 13x9x2-inch baking pan. Middle layer: melt ½ cup margarine. In mixing bowl combine melted margarine with creme de menthe. At low speed, beat in 3 cups powdered sugar mixture until smooth. Spread over chocolate layer and chill 1 hour. Top layer: melt remaining ¼ cup margarine with chocolate bits. Spread over mint layer. Chill 1 to 2 hours. Cut into squares. Store in refrigerator. Yields 36 bars.

Sally Brice-O'Hara

CHRISTMAS NUT THINS

1 cup sugar
1 cup butter
2 eggs, beaten
1½ cups flour

½ teaspoon salt
1 cup chopped nuts
1 teaspoon vanilla
Nut meats

Blend sugar and butter, add well beaten eggs. Sift flour and salt, add nuts and vanilla. Mix until smooth and light. Drop on greased baking sheet, spaced well apart. Place half a nut meat in center of each. Bake at 375 degrees 8 to 10 minutes. Yields 2 to 3 dozen.

Betty Shillen
Cold Springs, New Jersey

DANISH VANILLA WAFER

2½ cups flour
½ teaspoon baking powder
1 cup sugar

1 cup butter
2 egg yolks, slightly beaten
1 teaspoon lemon extract

Mix and sift flour, baking powder, and sugar. Cut butter into flour mixture. Stir in egg and lemon extract. Chill over night. Roll out 1/5 of dough at a time on lightly floured cloth. Roll dough to ⅛ inch thick. Cut out with favorite cookie cutters. Bake at 350 degrees for 8 to 10 minutes. Yields 2½ to 3 dozen. *Using Christmas cookie cutters, my mother made and hid these to be given out to family and friends every Christmas.*

Debra P. Chapman

CANADIAN SHORT BREAD

1 cup flour
½ cup butter
2 tablespoons sugar
2 eggs, beaten lightly

1½ cups brown sugar
1 cup walnuts or pecans
1 can of flaked coconut
½ teaspoon vanilla

Cream together first 3 ingredients. Pat into a greased 9x9-inch square pan. Bake at 350 degrees for 20 minutes. While baking combine the next 5 ingredients. When shortbread is done, spread this mixture over the top and continue baking for 10 minutes. Cut into bars while still warm. Yields 12 to 16 bars. *Delicious. Our mother baked this until her death at age 93.*

Caroline Baldt Mueller

TULIES AUX AMANDES

6 ounces sugar
½ ounce flour
2 eggs

6 ounces sliced almonds
Splash of vanilla

Mix eggs and sugar together. Beat lightly. Add flour, vanilla and almonds. You can add more almond slices if mixture seems too thin. Use greased cookie sheet or paper. Drop spoon sized and flatten with a wet fork. Bake at 375 degrees for 15 to 18 minutes. Makes a delicious crispy thin almond wafer.

Michel Gras, La Patisserie

RUM BALLS

5 cups crushed vanilla wafers
4 tablespoons cocoa
1 cup chopped walnuts

½ cup light corn syrup
½ cup rum
3 teaspoons water

Mix all ingredients and roll into balls. When they are dry, roll them in powdered sugar. Yields 3 to 4 dozen.

C. Karol

CHEWY CHOCOLATE-OATMEAL BARS

8 ounces cream cheese, softened
½ cup margarine
½ cup brown sugar, packed
¼ cup sugar
1 egg
1 teaspoon vanilla
1 cup quick oats, uncooked

⅔ cup flour
½ teaspoon baking powder
¼ teaspoon salt
6 ounces semi-sweet chocolate
  bits
¼ cup chopped nuts

Mix cream cheese, margarine and sugars together until well blended. Add egg and vanilla. Mix well. Add oats, flour, baking powder and salt. Mix well. Stir in chocolate bits and nuts. Pour into greased 13x9-inch baking pan. Bake at 350 degrees for 30 minutes. Cool and cut into bars. Yields 2 dozen 2 inch bars.

Brenda Williams-Elliott

CINNAMON FLATS

2 cups butter
2 cups sugar
4 cups flour

2 tablespoons cinnamon
2 egg yolks

Topping
2 egg whites beaten
1 cup sugar

1 tablespoon cinnamon
2 cups chopped pecans

Cream butter and sugar; add flour, cinnamon, and egg yolks. When blended, press lightly into jelly roll pan about ¼-inch thick. Beat egg whites slightly and brush over the surface. Mix sugar and cinnamon and sprinkle over egg whites. Sprinkle pecans overall pressing lightly. Bake at 350 degrees for 20 to 25 minutes. Yields 8 dozen.

Alice Linden, The Albert G. Stevens Inn

REFRIGERATOR MINT BARS

Bars

½ cup butter
1 (1-ounce) square unsweetened
   chocolate
¼ cup sugar
1 teaspoon vanilla

1 egg, beaten
1 cup shredded coconut
¼ cup old fashioned oats
½ cup chopped nuts
2 cups graham cracker crumbs

To Make Bars
Melt butter and chocolate in large saucepan over low heat. Add sugar, vanilla, egg, coconut, oats and nuts. Mix well. Add graham cracker crumbs. Press into greased 9-inch square baking pan.

Mint layer

¼ cup butter
1 tablespoon milk or cream
2 drops oil of peppermint, or

½ teaspoon peppermint extract
3 drops green food coloring
2 cups powdered sugar

For mint layer, melt butter in large saucepan and stir in milk, peppermint and food coloring. Add powdered sugar and mix well. Spread on bars.

Topping

½ (½-ounce) squares unsweetened
   chocolate
½ cup semi-sweet chocolate bits

For topping, melt unsweetened chocolate and semi-sweet chocolate bits in small saucepan over low heat. Spread over mint layer. Chill to allow chocolate to harden. Bring to room temperature and cut into small bars. If cut while cold chocolate will crack. Yields 12 to 16 bars.

Mary Suzanne Roehm
Grosse Pointe Woods, Michigan

SHEKERLACHMASA COOKIES

1 cup sweetened butter
Shortening

1½ cups sugar, blended until fine
2 cups flour

Melt butter over medium heat. Skim off salt foam. Pour into measuring cup and add shortening to make 1 cup. Cool. Beat on high speed until butter turns white. Add sugar and beat thoroughly. Add flour, 1 cup at a time, mixing well. Roll on lightly floured surface to ½-inch thickness. Cut into 2 inch strips. Place on ungreased baking sheet. Bake at 350 degrees for 8 to 10 minutes. Cool completely before removing from cookie sheet. Store in airtight container. Yields 3½ to 4 dozen. *Note:* I usually bake a couple of test cookies first. If top cracks, add a little more flour. If cookies flatten after baking, add chopped nuts and roll into balls to bake. Do not make cookies on a humid day! This is an Armenian, family recipe.

Mildred Spriggs

MINT FRANGOES

1 cup butter or margarine
2 cups sifted powdered sugar
4 squares chocolate, melted
4 eggs

2 teaspoons peppermint flavoring
2 teaspoons vanilla
1 cup vanilla wafers, crushed (½
   of 7 ounce box)

Beat butter and sugar until light and fluffy. Add chocolate and beat until smooth. Add 4 beaten eggs, beat again. Add flavoring, beat. Sprinkle ½ the crumbs in mini or small paper cups. Fill with chocolate mixture. Sprinkle remainder of crumbs on top. Freeze until needed. Yields 2 dozen. *A good dessert to keep on hand in freezer as refreshment with coffee or tea.*

Frances McDougal

DROP SAND TARTS

1½ cups butter
2 cups sugar
2 eggs

2 cups flour
Nutmeats

Beat in the order given. Cool dough (about 1 hour). Drop from teaspoon on ungreased cookie sheet. Place ½ nut meat on top or sprinkle with cinnamon and sugar. Bake at 375 degrees approximately 8 minutes. Remove from cookie sheet and cool. Yields 2½ to 3 dozens.

Betty Shillen
Cold Springs, New Jersey

CHINESE CHEWS

¾ cup flour
½ teaspoon baking powder
1 cup sugar
¼ teaspoon salt

1 cup finely cut dates
1 cup chopped walnuts
2 eggs

Mix ingredients and then pat into a large shallow buttered pan. Bake at 350 degrees for 20 minutes and cut at once into small squares and roll in granulated sugar. Store in a metal container. Yields 2½ to 3 dozen. *These cookies were always part of our Christmas.*

Caroline Badlt Mueller

COCONUT BARS

½ cup butter
1 cup graham crumbs
3½ ounces shredded coconut
6 ounces semi-sweet chocolate
   bits

6 ounces butterscotch chips
1 cup chopped nuts
1 can sweetened condensed milk

Use 13x9-inch pan. Melt butter in oven. Add graham crumbs, pat in pan. Spread coconut over graham crust. Add chocolate bits, butterscotch bits and nuts. Pour milk over top. Bake 350 degrees 30 minutes. Cut into bars while warm. Serves 10 to 15.

Dorothy Truman-Repman
New Castle, Delaware

PEANUT BUTTER FUDGE

2 cups sugar
1 tablespoon flour
3 to 6 tablespoons peanut butter
5 tablespoons butter

5 ounces (small can) evaporated
  milk
1 teaspoon vanilla

In heavy saucepan combine all ingredients, except vanilla, cook over medium heat until soft ball stage (ball forms when dropped in cold water). Add vanilla, remove from heat and beat until creamy. Pour into buttered dish. Cool. Yields 1½ to 2 pounds. *This is an old family recipe, from several generations. On a cold dreary day, it picks up everyone's spirits. Makes great Christmas gift.*

Joyce Smith
Medford, New Jersey

PEANUT BRITTLE

3 teaspoons baking soda
2 teaspoons water
2 teaspoons vanilla
3 cups sugar

2 cups water
2 cups light corn syrup
1 pound shelled roasted peanuts
6 tablespoons margarine

Combine soda, 2 teaspoons water, and vanilla. Set aside. Grease 3 (13x9-inch) baking sheets. In large saucepan combine sugar, 2 cups water and light corn syrup. Cook over medium heat to the soft ball stage or 240 degrees. Stir in peanuts and margarine. Stir constantly to 300 degrees. Remove from heat, stir in soda mixture. Pour equal amount onto each baking sheet. Cool. Yields 2 pounds.

Judy Bennett

SINFUL CHOCOLATE DESSERT

1 pound semi-sweet chocolate
  chunks
6 egg yolks (large)

¾ pounds sweet butter (at room
  temperature)
1 cup milk

Melt chocolate in milk in double boiler. Remove from heat and let cool about 5 minutes. Alternate egg yolks and butter into chocolate mixture. This is best done in a mixer. Mix just until incorporated. Turn into springform pan (wax paper in bottom, buttered sides). Bake in center of oven at 350 degrees for 25 minutes. Center will be almost liquid. Remove from oven, let cool partially. Put in refrigerator until completely cool. Remove pan sides, turn over onto plate. Remove pan bottom carefully. Top with whipped cream. Serves 10.

Bill and Rose Burns
Ridgewood, New Jersey

BLUEBERRY BUCKLE

¾ cup sugar
¼ cup soft shortening
1 egg
½ cup milk

2 teaspoons baking powder
½ teaspoon salt
2 cups flour
2 cups blueberries

Mix sugar, shortening, and egg together thoroughly. Stir in milk. Sift together and stir in flour, baking powder, and salt. Blend in, carefully, 2 cups washed blueberries. Spread batter in greased and floured 9-inch square pan. Bake at 375 degrees for 45 to 50 minutes. Serves 4 to 6. *Serve with whipped cream, ice cream or with milk and sugar.*

Nancy Byers

PEAR KUCHEN

¾ cup dark brown sugar
1 tablespoon flour
½ teaspoon ground cardamon
2 tablespoons butter
1 cup chopped unblanched almonds
1 cup sugar
3 eggs
1 teaspoon grated lemon peel

2 cups flour
1 teaspoon baking powder
1 teaspoon baking soda
1 teaspoon cardamon
¼ teaspoon salt
½ cup butter
1 cup sour cream
¾ pound pears, peeled and sliced

Mix first 5 ingredients and set aside for topping. Mix dry ingredients except sugar. Cream butter. Add sugar and eggs, one at a time. Mix in lemon peel. Stir in flour mixture alternately with sour cream. Mix until smooth. Grease and flour 13x9-inch pan. Pour cake batter in pan, place pears on top and cover with almond topping. Bake at 350 degrees for 45 minutes. Serve warm or cool with whipped cream if desired. Serves 2 to 4.

Joan Echevarria, Gingerbread House

PEACH CRUMBLE

1 (1-pound, 14-ounce) can cling peach slices
½ pound pecan shortbread cookies
1 tablespoon light brown sugar

1 teaspoon cinnamon
¼ cup butter
¼ cup chopped pecans
1 pint vanilla ice cream

Preheat oven to 400 degrees. Drain peaches and arrange in lightly greased 8-inch round baking dish. Place shortbread cookies in plastic bag and crush to fine crumbs with rolling pin. Add 1 tablespoon brown sugar and 1 teaspoon cinnamon. Sprinkle over peaches, dot with butter. Sprinkle with chopped pecans. Bake 8 to 10 minutes, at 350 degrees or until topping is bubbling. Serve warm with vanilla ice cream. Serves 6 to 8.

Charlotte Todd

NUT TORTE WITH COFFEE FILLING

6 eggs, separated
½ cup sugar
1¼ cups walnuts, ground fine

1½ teaspoons vanilla extract
2 heaping tablespoons bread
  crumbs

Cream egg yolks and sugar until light and creamy colored. Add nuts and vanilla. Mix thoroughly with bread crumbs and fold in stiffly beaten egg whites. Divide in half and pour into 2 well-buttered layer cake tins. Bake at 300 degrees for 25 to 30 minutes. Cool and fill with coffee filling. Serves 6 to 8.

Coffee Filling
¼ pound sweet butter
½ cup sugar

2 to 3 egg yolks
3 tablespoons very strong coffee

Cream butter and sugar, add yolks one by one, then add coffee a little at a time and blend thoroughly.

Ursula Ostromecki

RASPBERRY-LEMON RIBBON DESSERT

1 (3-ounce) package raspberry
  gelatin
1⅔ cups boiling water
1 (3-ounce) package lemon gelatin

1 (10-ounce) package frozen
  sweetened raspberries
1 cup ice cubes
⅓ cup instant non-fat dry milk

Dissolve raspberry gelatin in 1 cup boiling water in medium bowl. Dissolve lemon gelatin in remaining ⅔ cup boiling water in smaller mixing bowl. Add frozen raspberries to raspberry gelatin. Break up raspberries with fork until completely thawed, and gelatin is consistency of unbeaten egg white. Add ice cubes to lemon gelatin, stirring until gelatin is consistency of unbeaten egg white. Remove any remaining ice cubes. Add instant non-fat dry milk. Beat lemon mixture at high speed 2 to 3 minutes, or until fluffy. Spoon half of the raspberry mixture into a mold. Top with half of the lemon whipped mixture. Repeat. Chill several hours. Unmold and garnish with lemon slices. Serves 8 to 10.

Rosemary Hartman

CHOCOLATE MINT CREAM PUFFS

Cream Puffs

½ cup butter

¼ teaspoon salt

1 cup flour

4 eggs

Place 1 cup water, butter and salt in saucepan. Bring to a boil. Remove from heat, add flour all at once. Beat with a wooden spoon until flour is incorporated. Return to heat and keep beating until dough is thick and leaves the sides of the pan. Remove pan from heat and beat in eggs one at a time. Pre-heat oven to 425 degrees. Drop dough by tablespoons or teaspoons on ungreased baking sheet. Bake approximately 30 minutes or until brown. Turn off oven and prick the puffs. Leave in 10 minutes to dry. While the puffs are cooking make the chocolate mint mousse filling. Serves 12 to 24.

Ann Miller

CHOCOLATE MINT MOUSSE FILLING

4 tablespoons chopped fresh
 peppermint

½ cup boiling water

2 ounces unsweetened chocolate

1 ounce bittersweet chocolate

3 egg whites

1 cup sugar

2 cups heavy cream

½ teaspoon vanilla

Steep mint in boiling water for 30 minutes. Strain into top of double boiler. Add the chocolate and melt over warm water. Beat egg whites until stiff, gradually adding sugar. Beat until thick meringue forms. Whip cream. fold whipped cream, cooled chocolate mixture and vanilla into beaten egg whites. Fill puffs. (Lift out a little piece to make a hole in the puff.) Freeze on baking sheet until firm. When ready to serve, put one large or 3 small on plate and cover with chocolate mint sauce. Yields filling for 12 to 24 cream puffs.

Ann Miller

CHOCOLATE MINT SAUCE

¼ cup boiling water
2 tablespoons chopped fresh mint
9 ounces semi-sweet chocolate

1½ ounces unsweetened chocolate
1 tablespoons butter
½ cup milk

Steep mint 30 minutes. Strain. Melt chocolate and butter in double boiler over hot water. Stir in milk and 2 tablespoons of mint "tea." Stir until well blended. Serve warm. May decorate with sugared mint leaves, made by washing and drying mint leaves well. Brush leaves with beaten egg white and dip in superfine granulated sugar. Dry on wax paper. Store between layers of wax paper in a covered tin. Yields about 1 cup.

Ann Miller

APPLE CRISP

4 cups apples, peeled and sliced
¼ cup water
1 teaspoon cinnamon
¾ cup flour

1 cup granulated sugar
½ teaspoon salt
½ cup margarine

Put apples and water in glass pie plate or 10x6-inch baking dish. Sift flour, cinnamon, salt and sugar together. cut in margarine until consistency of coarse crumbs. Spread on top of apples. Bake 350 degrees for 40 minutes. Serve warm or cool. Serves 4 to 6. *Easy and can be made ahead.*

Nancy Byers

VIRGINIA APPLE PUDDING

½ cup butter
1 cup sugar
1 cup flour
2 teaspoons baking powder

¼ teaspoon cinnamon
¼ teaspoon salt
1 cup milk
2 cups cooked apples

Melt butter in 2-quart casserole. Combine next six ingredients, pour over butter. Drain apples; pile in center of batter. Bake in moderate oven, 375 degrees for 30 to 40 minutes or until batter covers fruit and crust becomes brown. Serve hot with cream or ice cream. Serves 4 to 6.

Tom Williams

BLACKBERRY MUSH

l quart blackberries
l cup water
l cup sugar

3 tablespoons cornstarch
l tablespoon water

Wash blackberries and drain. Add water and cook until berries are tender, about 10 minutes. Strain to remove seeds if desired, reserving cooking water. Return to pan, heat, add sugar and bring to boil. Add enough cornstarch, moistened with l tablespoon water, to thicken. Cook, stirring, about 8 minutes. Remove from heat, cool and chill. Serve plain or with whipped cream. Serves 6. *This recipe appeared in the Philly Evening Bulletin 7/27/33. It is a good plain summer dessert, but not generally included with today's recipes.*

Fran McDougal

BREAD PUDDING WITH WHISKEY SAUCE

l (10-ounce) loaf stale French
  bread or 8 cups any bread,
  stale
4 cups milk or 2 cups milk and 2
  cups heavy cream
2 cups sugar
4 tablespoons melted butter

3 eggs
2 tablespoons vanilla
l cup chopped pecans
l cup shredded coconut (optional)
l teaspoon cinnamon
l teaspoon nutmeg

Combine all ingredients. Mixture should be very moist but not sloppy. Pour into 9x9-inch baking dish. Place on middle rack in preheated oven at 350 degrees for 1¼ hours until top is golden brown. Serve with Sauce. Serves 6.

Whiskey Sauce
½ cup butter
1½ cups powdered sugar

l egg
½ cup bourbon (less to taste)

Cream butter and sugar over medium heat until all butter is absorbed. Remove from heat. Blend in egg. Pour in bourbon gradually to taste stirring constantly. Sauce will thicken as it cools to warm. Serve warm over warm pudding.

Steve Miller and Janet Merwin, 410 Bank Street Restaurant

FRUIT CREAM

4 cups cranberries
3½ cups water
1½ cups sugar

1 stick cinnamon
2 cloves
3 heaping tablespoons cornstarch

Combine berries with water, boil 5 minutes, and press through a sieve. Reserve ½ of the liquid and allow to cool. Combine the rest with the sugar, cinnamon and cloves, and simmer another 10 minutes. Discard cinnamon and cloves. Dissolve cornstarch in the cooled part of the liquid and pour into the boiling part. Stir continuously for 2 minutes. Wet a mold, sprinkle with sugar and pour fruit cream into it. Chill and allow to thicken. Serve with heavy cream. Serves 6. *Can be made ahead of time.*

Ursula Ostromecki

CHERRY CREAM CHEESE TURNOVERS

1 (8-ounce) pack cream cheese
1 cup butter
1 teaspoon vanilla
2 cups sifted flour

Pinch of salt
1 can cherry pie filling
Powdered sugar

Blend the cream cheese and butter. Stir in vanilla. Add flour and salt and mix well. Place in refrigerator for 1 hour. Roll out on a floured surface and cut into 2-inch squares. Place 2 cherries from cherry pie filling in center of each square. Fold over and seal edges. Place on a baking sheet. Bake at 350 degrees for about 25 minutes. Cool and dust with powdered sugar. Yields 20 turnovers. *A good bite size pass-around dessert.*

Charlotte Todd

CHERRY BLOSSOM CHEESE TARTS

16 ounces cream cheese
½ cup sugar
2 eggs

2 teaspoons vanilla
18 vanilla wafers
1 can cherry pie filling

Beat cream cheese, sugar, eggs and vanilla at medium speed. Put paper cupcake liners in muffin tins. Place 1 vanilla wafer in each liner; then fill them with mixture to about ¼ from top. Bake for 12 to 15 minutes in a 350 degree oven. When cool, spoon the cherry pie filling on top; place tarts in refrigerator to cool. When ready to serve, tarts may be garnished with whipped cream. Serves 18. *Do not overbake or you will lose the cheese texture. Taken from Favorite Recipes Felician Sisters Our Lady of the Angels Convent, Enfield, Connecticut.*

Stella Lilla

CHARLESTON HUGUENOT TORTE

4 eggs
3 cups sugar
8 tablespoons flour
½ teaspoon salt

2 cups chopped tart cooking
  apples
2 cups chopped pecans

Topping
Whipped cream

Ground Nuts

Beat whole eggs in electric mixer bowl or with rotary beater until frothy and lemon colored. Add rest of ingredients in above order. Pour into two well buttered baking pans about 12x8-inch. Bake at 325 degrees about 45 minutes. Should look crusty and brown. Cut, lift with turner. Serve with whipped cream and ground nuts. Serves 16. *Always served to special guests by the proper Charlestonian hostess.*

Ann Miller

MOTHER WILLIS' HOLIDAY PUDDING

1 teaspoon salt
1 cup sugar
1 cup suet, chopped
2 cups flour
½ cup milk
2 teaspoons baking powder
1 cup raisins
½ cup sugar

1 cup water
1 tablespoon flour
1 cup water
1 tablespoon flour
1 tablespoon butter
1 teaspoon vanilla
½ teaspoon almond extract

Mix the first 7 ingredients until a thick dough forms. Place dough in a clean cotton bag and tie closed. Boil for 1½ hours. While this is boiling make sauce by placing sugar, water, flour and butter in small saucepan. Cook until creamy. Remove from heat, let cool, then add vanilla and almond extract. Serve pudding hot with sauce poured over it. Serves 4 to 6. *This pudding has been handed down for generations—a holiday tradition. Candied fruit may be added to pudding.*

R. Richard Willis
Lake Hopatcong, New Jersey

HOT FUDGE PUDDING

1½ cups buttermilk biscuit baking
  mix
½ cup sugar
½ to 1 cup chopped nuts
½ cup milk

½ cup brown sugar
1½ cups boiling water
6-ounce package semi-sweet
  chocolate bits

Heat oven to 350 degrees. Mix baking mix, sugar, nuts and milk. Turn batter into greased 2-quart baking dish. Sprinkle with brown sugar. Pour water over chocolate bits in a bowl. Let stand 1 or 2 minutes until bits melt, then stir until blended. Pour over batter. Bake 40 to 45 minutes. Let stand 5 minutes to cool. During baking the pudding will rise to top of dish and sauce will form at bottom. Invert on serving plate, drip sauce on top. Serves 6 to 8. *You can add whipped cream on top. A very unusual dessert, always enjoyed by all.*

Darlene Orminski

222

Index

Christiana Campbells
Duke of Glosester

Cascades restaurant

A
ACCOMPANIMENTS
Bacon Scallion Dressing 167
Baked Pineapple 165
Beechmont Granola 166
Garlic Mint Dressing 169
Hot Mustard 170
Jelly (See Separate Listings)
Lemon Butter 171
Pineapple Pudding 167
Pumpkin Shell Casserole 174
Quark 166
Sauce (See Separate Listings)
Scalloped Apples 174
Shoe Peg Relish 175
Spring Compote 176
Sweet Bell Pepper Jam 176
Vanilla Extract 177
Wine Whipped Cream 177
Almond Cookies (Tuiles Aux
   Amandes) 208
Alsatin Braised Sauerkraut 141
APPETIZERS
Cold
Chicken Salad Balls 13
Chili-Cheese Pinwheels 14
Pickled Herring 20
Pickled Mushrooms 20
Stuffed Bread 25
Dip
Chili Con Quesco Dip 13
Chili Dip 14
Curry Dip 16
Dill'N Onion Dip 17
Marimba Dip 17
Shrimp Dip 24
Veggie Dip 26
Hot
Artichoke Hearts 9
Artichoke Nibbles 10
Bacon Wrapped Chicken Livers ... 9
Cheese Cookies 11
Chicken Nuggets 12
Chicken Sticks 13
Clam Pie 15
Crab Canapes 15
Crab Meat Puffs 16
Croustades Aux Champignons ... 21
Glazed Chicken Wings 12
Meat Ball Appetizers 18
Olive Cheddar Nugget Snacks ... 21
Onion Strips 22
Party Meatballs 18
Party Rye Slices 22

Peroski 22
Seafood Canapes 24
Stilton or Blue Cheese Wafers ... 25
Stuffed Mushrooms 19
Swiss Cheese Puffs 26
Molds & Spreads
Barbara Gordon's Cheese
   Appetizer 10
Christmas Cheese Ball 9
Crab Spread 16
Curry Pate 17
Delicious Cheese Ring 11
Holiday Cheese Balls 11
Salmon Mold 23
Salmon Mousse 23
Shrimp Butter 25
Tangy Spread 26
Corn Crisps 15
APPLES
Apple Cake 202
Apple Candy Pie 185
Apple Crisp 218
Apple Crumb Pie 185
Apple Onion Sauce 165
Apples 'N Stuffing Pork Chops., .. 135
Fried Ham with Apples 136
Jewish Apple Cake 192
Scalloped Apples 174
Virginia Apple Pudding 218
APRICOT
Apricot Delight Pie 186
Granola Muffins 79
Loin of Pork Apricot 134
Sparkling Apricot Pineapple
   Punch 27
ARTICHOKE
Artichoke Hearts 9
Artichoke Nibbles 10
Artichoke Rice Salad 43
Chicken-Ham Artichoke
   Casserole 106
Geoff and Bobbie's Spinach
   Terrific 153
Pasta Salad 72
Shrimp and Artichoke Hearts En
   Casserole 102
Spinach and Artichoke Bake 152
Spinach Artichoke Casserole 153
Spinach Casserole 153
ASPARAGUS
Asparagus Omelette 65
Asparagus Vichyssoise 35
Asparagus with Orange Hollandaise
   Sauce 141

INDEX

Aunt Bettinas' Carrots 144
Aunt Olga's Pound Cake 201

B

BACON
Bacon and Cheese Puff 63
Bacon Scallion Dressing 167
Bacon Wrapped Chicken Livers 9
Canadian Bacon Eggs 66
Governor's Egg Casserole 66
Baked Chicken Salad 107
Baked Flounder 89
Baked Pineapple 165
Baltimore Inn Deviled Clams 89
BANANA
Banana-Caramel Pie 186
Banana Cream Coffee Cake 203
Banana Split Sundae Pie 187
Chocolate Banana Creme Pie 188
Mandarin Orange Pie 190
Quick and Easy Banana Bread ... 77
Barbara Gordon's Cheese Appetizer . 10
BARBECUE
Chicken Barbecue Sauce 167
Ham Bar-B-Q's 57
Summer's Barbecue Sauce 176
Barbecued Chicken Lea Ming 107
Beach Plum Jelly 165
BEAN(S) (Also See Chili)
Bean Casserole 142
Green Beans (See Separate Listings)
Three Bean Salad 54
Beechmont Granola 166
Beechmont Shirred Eggs 65
BEEF
Beef in Sherry 128
Beef Roll-Ups 125
Beef Stock Lentil Soup 39
Carefree Stew 125
Chinese Casserole 125
Chipped Beef Casserole 69
Easy Beef Bourguignonne 132
Hache 129
Hannah's Homemade Soup 37
Italian Roast Beef 131
Marinated Tenderloin 129
Pepper Steak 127
Sherried Beef 132
Steak Romano 124
Sukiyaki 131
Vegetable Soup 42
Windsor Baked Steak 126
BEEF, GROUND
Bean Casserole 142

Christy's Chili 130
Jim's Favorite Chili 130
Meat Balls (See Separate Listings)
Reuben Meatloaf 128
Spaghetti Superb 74
Taco Salad 55
Beer Bread (Easy) 77
Beer Cheese Fondue 63
Beets Harvard 142
Better Than--Cake 199
BEVERAGES
Chocolate Irish Cream 29
Holiday Eggnog 30
Margueritas 29
Orange Eggnog 32
Punch (See Separate Listings)
Rum Slush 31
Super Cider Float 32
Swedish Christmas Glogg 31
Bisque, Crab 36
Black Eyed Peas, New Year's Day .. 160
Black Walnut Pie 187
Blackberry Mush 219
Bleu Cheese Deviled Eggs 66
Blue Cheese or Stilton Wafers ... 25
BLUEBERRY
Blueberry Bread 77
Blueberry Brunch Cake 202
Blueberry Buckle 214
BREADS
Muffins, Granola 79
Muffins, Sweet Potato 82
Pancakes, Pop 86
Quick
Blueberry Bread 77
Cranberry Nut Bread 78
Coconut Bread 78
(Easy) Beer Bread 77
Herb Bread 79
Irish Soda Bread 81
Pumpkin Bread 80
Quick and Easy Banana Bread .. 77
Quick Whole Wheat Bread 83
Shortcut Monkey Bread 80
Southern Spoon Bread 82
Sweet Potato Bread 83
Yogurt Bread 84
Rolls, Quick Sour Cream 81
Toast, Colvmns Peach 85
Toast, French 84
Waffles, Sour Cream 85
Bread Pudding with Whiskey Sauce 219
BROCCOLI
Broccoli Casserole 143

Broccoli Mold 143
Broccoli Salad 46
Broccoli Supreme 144
Curry Chicken with Broccoli 113
Green Rice 161
BRUNCH
Blueberry Brunch Cake 202
Mincemeat, Brunch Cake 195
Oven Omelette Brunch 67
Butter Crumb Coffee Cake 204
Butter, Lemon 171
Butter, Shrimp 25
Butterflied Leg of Lamb 132

C
Cabbage (See Also Slaw)
CAKE
Apple Cake 202
Aunt Olga's Pound Cake 201
Better Than--Cake 199
Blueberry Brunch Cake 202
Carrot, Raisin Prune Cake 200
Cheese Cake (See Separate Listing)
Chess Cake 195
Creme De Menthe Cake Squares . 205
Coconut Carrot Cake 197
Coffee Cake (See Separate Listing)
Cranberry Cake 196
Dundee (White Fruit) Cake 199
Fudge Pudding Cake 194
Funny Cake 194
Grace Gilman's Gingerbread 203
Hawaiian Wedding Cake 192
Jewish Apple Cake 192
Mandarin Orange Pineapple Cake 191
Mincemeat Brunch Cake 195
1-2-3-4 Cake 198
Prune Cake 205
Rum Cake 204
Walnut Rum Cake 206
Victorian Currant Cakes 201
California Vegetable Medley 157
Canadian Baconed Eggs 66
Canadian Short Bread 208
CANDY
Peanut Brittle 213
Peanut Butter Fudge 213
Cape May Cole Slaw 52
Caramel-Banana Pie 186
Carefree Stew 125
CARROT(S)
Aunt Betina's Carrots 144
Carrot, Raisin, Prune Cake 200
Coconut Carrot Cake 197

Marinated Carrot Sticks 144
Mashed (Smashed) Carrots 145
Cashew Chicken 108
CASSEROLE
Meat/Main Dish
Chicken Casserole 112
Chicken-Ham Artichoke
Casserole 106
Chinese Casserole 125
Chipped Beef Casserole 69
Fish Casserole 94
Governor's Egg Casserole 66
Pumpkin Shell Casserole 174
Quick Chicken Casserole 106
Shrimp and Artichoke Heart's En
Casserole 102
Shrimp and Cheese Casserole ... 102
Shrimp Casserole 101
Shrimp Casserole Surprise 103
Three "C" Casserole 114
Vegetable
Bean Casserole 142
Broccoli Casserole 143
Eggplant Casserole 146
Lima Bean Casserole 148
Mashed Potato Zucchini
Casserole 151
Mixed Vegetable Casserole 156
Mushroom Casserole 147
Rice Casserole 162
Sherried Sweet Potato Casserole 151
Spinach Artichoke Casserole 153
Spinach Casserole 153
Spinach Casserole 154
Cauliflower Salad 47
Celery Soup 35
Champagne Punch 27
Charleston Hugenot Torte 221
Cheddar Puff 63
Cheddar Nugget Snacks, Olive ... 21

CHEESE (See Separate Cheese and Eggs
and Cheese Listings)
Bacon and Cheese Puffs 63
Barbara Gordon's Cheese Appetizer 10
Beer Cheese Fondue 63
Cheese Cookies 11
Cheese Dreams 56
Cherry Blossom Cheese Tarts 221
Chili-Cheese Pinwheels 14
Christmas Cheese Balls 9
Creamy Macaroni and Cheese 70
Delicious Cheese Ring 11

INDEX

Holiday Cheese Balls 11
Hot Ham and Cheese Sandwich ... 56
Pecan Cheese Pie 184
Shrimp and Cheese Casserole 102
Cheese Cake, Easy 198
Cherry Blossom Cheese Tarts 221
Cherry Cream Cheese Turnovers ... 220
Chess Cake 195
Chewy Chocolate Oatmeal Bars ... 209

CHICKEN
Baked Chicken Salad 107
Barbecued Chicken Lea Ming 107
Cashew Chicken 108
Chicken and Stuffing Strata 108
Chicken Barbecue Sauce 167
Chicken Breasts Marsala 109
Chicken Breasts Veronique 109
Chicken Cacciatore 111
Chicken Casserole 112
Chicken Dijon 105
Chicken Divan 111
Chicken Divine 110
Chicken Fiesta 110
Chicken-Ham Artichoke
  Casserole 106
Chicken in Raspberry Cream 121
Chicken in Red Wine Vinegar ... 120
Chicken in Sherry Sauce 120
Chicken Kiev 121
Chicken Livers, Bacon Wrapped 9
Chicken Nuggets 12
Chicken Pecan Quiche 105
Chicken Pesto 112
Chicken Salad Balls 13
Chicken Salad Habana 48
Chicken Saltimbocca 120
Chicken Sticks 13
Chicken Tamale 119
Choice Chicken Bake 114
Cobb Salad 44
Cold Chicken Curry 123
Crispy Peppery Chicken 119
Crunchy Drumsticks 118
Curry Chicken with Broccoli 113
Glazed Chicken Wings 12
Hungarian Noodles 69
Jake's Chicken 118
Mainstay Chicken Pie 113
Molded Chicken Salad 49
Moo Goo Gai Pien 117
Old Fashioned Chicken Pot Pie ... 117
One Pan Paella 122
Oven Baked Sesame Chicken 106
Overnight Layered Chicken Salad · 47

Quick Chicken Casserole 106
Quickie Chickie 116
Ranger Chicken 116
Red Chicken Jambalaya 115
Soy Chicken Salad 48
Sukiyaki 131
Sweet and Sour Chicken 115
Sweet Spicy Chicken Breast 122
Three "C" Casserole 114

CHILI
Chili-Cheese Pinwheels 14
Chili Con Quesco Dip 13
Chili Dip 14
Cristy's Chili 130
Jim's Favorite 130
Chinese Casserole 125
Chinese Chews 212
Chipped Beef Casserole 69

CHOCOLATE (See Also Fudge)
Chewy Chocolate-Oatmeal Bars . 209
Chocolate Banana Creme Pie 188
Chocolate Butternut Sauce 178
Chocolate Irish Cream 29
Chocolate Mint Cream Puffs 217
Chocolate Mint Mousse Filling ... 217
Chocolate Mint Sauce 218
Coconut Bars 212
French Silk Pie .... .189
Funny Cake 194
Mint Frangoes 211
Refrigerator Mint Bars 210
Rum Balls 208
Sinful Chocolate Dessert 214

CHOWDER
Fish Chowder 36
Manhattan Clam Chowder 38
Nassau Seafood Chowder 42
New England Corn Chowder 38
Seafood Chowder 41
Choice Chicken Bake 114
Cholesterol-Free Cole Slaw 52
Christmas Cheese Ball 9
Christmas Nut Thins 207
Christmas Salad 43
Christy's Chili 130
Cider Float, Super 32
Cinnamon Flats 209

CLAMS
Baltimore Inn Deviled Clams ... 89
Clam Pie 15
Clam Sauce 90
Down Jersey Clam Pie 92
Manhattan Clam Chowder 38
One Pan Paella 122

Classic Crab Imperial 91
Cobb Salad 44
COCONUT
  Coconut Bars 212
  Coconut Bread 78
  Coconut Carrot Cake 197
  Coconut Cream Frosting 197
  Coconut Pie Crust 188
  Ice Cream Pie 190
Coffee (See Mocha)
COFFEE CAKE
  Banana Cream Coffee Cake 203
  Buttered Crumb Coffee Cake 204
  Coffee Cake 198
  Honey Twist Coffee Cake 193
Coffee Filling for Nut Torte 216
Cold Chicken Curry 123
Colvmns Peach Toast 85
COOKIES
  Bar
    Canadian Short Bread 208
    Chewy Chocolate Oatmeal-Bars . 209
    Chinese Chews 212
    Cinnamon Flats 209
    Coconut Bars 212
    Creme De Menthe Squares 206
    Refrigerator Mint Bars 210
  Drop
    Christmas Nut Thins 207
    Drop Sand Tarts 212
    Tuiles Aux Amandes 208
  Molded or Shaped
    Danish Vanilla Wafers 207
    Mint Frangoes 211
    Rum Balls 208
    Shekerlachmasa Cookies 211
CORN
  Broccoli Supreme 144
  Corn Crisps 15
  Country Style Corn Pudding 145
  Huntington Corn Pudding 145
  New England Corn Chowder 38
Cornish Hens, Holiday 123
Country Style Corn Pudding 145
CRAB
  Classic Crab Imperial 91
  Crab and Rice Ramekins 90
  Crab Bisque 36
  Crab Canapes 15
  Crab Imperial 91
  Crab Meat Puffs 16
  Crab Quiche 92
  Crab Spread 16
  Herb Dumpling on Baked Crab ... 96

Seafood Rarebit Souffle 100
CRANBERRY(IES)
  Cranberry Cake 196
  Cranberry Cake Frosting 196
  Cranberry Nut Bread 78
  Cranberry Wine Jelly 168
  Fruit Cream 220
Cream Cheese Turnovers, Cherry .. 220
Cream of Mushroom Soup 36
Cream of Parsnip Soup 39
Cream of Peanut Soup 39
Cream Puffs, Chocolate Mint 217
Creamy Macaroni and Cheese 70
Creamy Summer Slaw 53
Creme De Menthe Cake Squares ... 205
Creme De Menthe Squares 206
CREOLE
  Creole Green Beans 142
  Eggplant Creole 147
  Poached Fish Creole 97
  Shrimp Creole 103
Crispy Peppery Chicken 119
Crispy Pickle Slices 168
Croustades Aux Champignons 21
Crunchy Drumsticks 118
Cucumber (Also See Pickles)
Cucumber Mousse 45
Currant Cakes, Victorian 201
CURRY
  Cold Chicken Curry 123
  Curry Chicken with Broccoli 113
  Curry Dip 16
  Curry Pate 17
  Seafood with Curry Sauce 100

D
Danish Vanilla Wafers 207
Delicious Cheese Ring 11
DESSERT
  Apple Crisp 218
  Blackberry Mush 219
  Blueberry Buckle 214
  Cakes (See Separate Listings)
  Charleston Huguenot Torte 221
  Cherry Blossom Cheese Tarts 221
  Cherry Cream Cheese Turnovers . 220
  Chocolate Mint Cream Puffs 217
  Chocolate Mint Mousse Filling ... 217
  Cookies (See Separate Listings)
  Fruit Cream 220
  Nut Torte with Coffee Filling 216
  Peach Crumble 215
  Pear Kuchen 215
  Pies (See Separate Listings)

INDEX

Pudding (See Separate Listings)
Raspberry-Lemon Ribbon Dessert . 216
Sauce (See Separate Listings)
Sinful Chocolate Dessert 214
Deviled Clams, Baltimore Inn 89
Deviled Eggs, Bleu Cheese 66
Dill Sauce 169
Dill 'N Onion Dip 17
Down Jersey Clam Pie 92
Drop Sand Tarts 212
Dude Ranch Meatball Bake 129
Dumpling on Baked Crab, Herb 96
Dundee (White Fruit) Cake 199

E

E-Z Fish Florentine 94
Easy Beef Bourguignonne 132
(Easy) Beer Bread 77
Easy Cheese Cake 198
Easy Turkey Tetrazzini 124
Easy Veal Marsala 137
Eggnog, Holiday 30
Eggnog, Orange 32
Eggplant Casserole 146
Eggplant Creole 147
EGGS (Also See Eggs and Cheese Quiche)
  Beechmont Shirred Eggs 65
  Bleu Cheese Deviled Eggs 66
  Canadian Baconed Eggs 66
  Oeufs Bercy 68
  Oven Omelette Brunch 67
  Scotch Eggs 67
EGGS AND CHEESE
  Asparagus Omelette 65
  Governor's Egg Casserole 66
  Sausage Strata 64
English Fish and Chips 93
ENTREES (See Beef, Ham, Lamb, Pork,
  Poultry and Veal)
"Erwten Soup" 40
Extract, Vanilla 177

F

Filling, Coffee 216
Filling, Chocolate Mint Mousse 217
FISH (Also See Flounder, Rockfish, Salmon
  and Tuna)
  E-Z Fish Florentine 94
  English Fish and Chips 93
  Fish Casserole 94
  Fish Chowder 36
  Fish Fillets with Mustard-Caper
    Sauce 93
  Poached Fish Creole 97

Seafood Brochette 99
Seafood Canapes 24
Seafood Chowder 41
Flaky Pie Crust 191
Florentine, E-Z Fish 94
Florida Sunshine Punch 30
FLOUNDER
  Baked Flounder 89
  Fish Fillets with Mustard Caper
    Sauce 93
  Flounder in Foil 94
  Flounder in Spinach 95
  Flounder Parmesan 95
Fondue, Beer Cheese 63
French Onion Soup 37
French Silk Pie 189
French Toast 84
Fried Ham with Apples 136
Fritos, Homemade (Corn Crisps) 15
Fritters, Oyster 98
Frosting, Coconut Cream 197
Frosting, Cranberry Cake 196
FRUIT (Also See Individual Fruit Listings
  and Salads: Fruit)
  Dundee (With Fruit) Cake 199
  Fruit Cream 220
  Spring Compote 176
FUDGE
  Fudge Pie 189
  Fudge Pudding Cake 194
  Hot Fudge Pudding 222
  Hot Fudge Sauce 170
  Marshmallow Fudge Sauce 172
  Mud Pie 188
  Peanut Butter Fudge 213
Funny Cake 194

G

Garden Pasta Salad 72
Garlic Mint Dressing 169
Geoff and Bobbie's Spinach Terrific . 153
German Pudding Sauce 169
Ginger Pear Salad 51
Gingerbread, Grace Gilman's 203
Glazed Chicken Wings 12
Governor's Egg Casserole 66
Grace Gilman's Gingerbread 203
GRAINS (See Rice)
Grandma Egelhoff's Pineapple Cream
  Salad 27
Granola, Beechmont 166
Granola Muffins 79
Grasshopper Pie 181

GREEN BEANS
Creole Green Beans 142
Green Bean and Potato Salad 45
Green Rice 161
Green Noodles 71
Green Tomato Pie 154

H
Hache 129
HAM
Broccoli Mold 143
Fried Ham with Apples 136
Ham and Cheese Bake 64
Ham Bar-B-Q's 57
Chicken-Ham Artichoke
Casserole 106
Chicken Saltimbocca 120
Hot Ham and Cheese Sandwich ... 56
Marimba Dip 17
Oeufs Bercy 68
Sherried Ham 136
Vegetable Strata 157
Hannah's Homemade Soup 37
Harvard Beets 142
Hawaiian Wedding Cake 192
Hearts of Palm Salad 44
Herb Bread 79
Herb Dumpling on Baked Crab 96
Herring, Pickled 20
Holiday Cheese Balls 11
Holiday Cornish Hens 123
Holiday Eggnog 30
Holiday Potato Dish 150
HOLLANDAISE
Hollandaise Sauce 170
Mock Hollandaise Sauce 173
Hollandaise Sauce with Asparagus 141
Honey Twist Coffee Cake 193
Hot Dog Stew 137
Hot Fudge Pudding 22
Hot Fudge Sauce 170
Hot Ham and Cheese Sandwich 56
Hot Mushroom Hors D' Oeuvres ... 19
Hot Mustard 170
Hungarian Noodles 69
Huntington Corn Pudding 145

I
Ice Box Cucumber Pickles 171
Ice Cream Pie 190
Inside-Out Sandwiches 57
Irish Cream, Chocolate 29
Irish Soda Bread 81
Italian Roast Beef 131

J
Jake's Chicken 118
Jam, Sweet Bell Pepper 176
Jambalaya, Red Chicken 115
Jambalaya, Shrimp 104
JELLY
Beach Plum Jelly 165
Cranberry Wine Jelly 168
Pepper Jelly 173
Jewish Apple Cake 192
Jezebel's Sauce 171
Jim's Favorite Chili 130

K
Kentucky Hot Browns 58
Kuchen, Pear 215

L
LAMB
Butterflied Leg of Lamb 132
Lamb Meatballs with Yogurt
Sauce 133
Rack of Lamb Moutarde 133
Lasagna, Vegetable 158
LEMON
Lemon Butter 171
Lemon Cream Pie 190
Lemon Fluff Pie 182
Lemon Sauce 172
Queen Victoria's Coronation Tart .. 182
Raspberry-Lemon Ribbon Dessert . 216
Lentil Soup, Beef Stock 39
Lima Bean Casserole 148
Liverwurst, Stuffed Bread 25
Lobster in Tomato Sauce 97
Loin of Pork Apricot 134
Lulu Salad 49

M
MACARONI
Chipped Beef Casserole 69
Creamy Macaroni and Cheese 70
Matchless Macaroni Salad 70
Shrimp Casserole Surprise 103
Mainstay Chicken Pie 113
Make Ahead Mashed Potatoes 149
Mandarin Orange Pie 190
Mandarin Orange Pineapple Cake . 191
Mandarin Pork and Vegetable 134
Manhattan Clam Chowder 38
Margueritas 29
Marimba Dip 17
Marinated Carrot Sticks 144
Marinated Tenderloin 129

INDEX

Marshmallow Fudge Sauce 172
Mashed (Smashed) Carrots 145
Mashed Potato Zucchini Casserole .. 151
Matchless Macaroni Salad 70
Mayonnaise, Spicy 175
MEAT BALLS
  Meatball Appetizers 18
  Dude Ranch Meatball Bake 129
  Lamb Meatballs with Yogurt
    Sauce 133
  Party Meatballs 18
Meatloaf, Reuben 128
Mincemeat Brunch Cake 195
MINT
  Chocolate Mint Creme Puffs 217
  Chocolate Mint Mousse Filling ... 217
  Chocolate Mint Sauce 218
  Garlic Mint Dressing 169
  Mint Frangoes 211
Mixed Vegetable Casserole 156
Mocha Angel Pie 181
Mocha Milk Punch 28
Mock Hollandaise Sauce 173
Molded Chicken Salad 49
Monkey Bread, Shortcut 80
Moo Goo Gai Pien 117
Mother Willis' Holiday Pudding ... 222
Mother's Potato Salad 50
MOUSSE
  Cucumber Mousse 45
  Chocolate Mint Mousse Filling ... 217
  Salmon Mousse 23
Mud Pie 188
Muffins, Granola 79
Muffins, Sweet Potato 82
Mush, Blackberry 219
MUSHROOM(S)
  Cream of Mushroom Soup 36
  Croustades Aux Champignons 21
  Hot Mushroom Hors D'Oeuvres ... 19
  Mushroom Casserole 147
  Mushrooms Florentine 148
  Pickled Mushrooms 20
  Stuffed Mushrooms 19
Mustard, Hot 170

N
Nassau Seafood Chowder 42
New England Corn Chowder 38
New Year's Day Black-Eyed Peas .. 160
Newburg, Seafood 100
NOODLES
  Chicken Cacciatore 111
  Green Noodles 71
  Hungarian Noodles 69
  Norfolk Noodles 71
Norfolk Noodles 71
NUT(S) (Also See Separate Listings)
  Christmas Nut Thins 207
  Nut Torte with Coffee Filling 216

O
Oatmeal Bars, Chewy Chocolate ... 209
Oeufs Bercy 68
Old-Fashioned Chicken Pot Pie 117
Olive Cheddar Nugget Snacks 21
Omelette, Asparagus 65
Omelette, Oven Omelette Brunch ... 67
1-2-3-4 Cake 198
One Pan Paella 122
ONION
  Apple Onion Sauce 165
  Dill'N Onion Dip 17
  French Onion Soup 37
  Onion Strips 22
ORANGE (Also See Mandarin Orange)
  Asparagus with Orange Hollandaise
    Sauce 141
  Orange Cream Fruit Salad 50
  Orange Eggnog 32
Oven Baked Sesame Chicken 106
Oven-Crisp Potatoes 152
Oven Omelette Brunch 67
Overnight Layered Chicken Salad .. 47
Overnight Tossed Salad 54
OYSTER(S)
  Down Jersey Clam Pie 92
  Oyster Fritters 98
  Ribbon Oyster Stew 96
  Scalloped Oysters 99

P
Paella, One Pan 122
Pancakes, Pop 86
Parmesan, Flounder 95
Parsnip Soup, Cream of 39
Party Meatballs 18
Party Rye Slices 22
PASTA (Also See Separate Pasta Listings)
  Pasta Primivera 73
  Pasta Salad 72
Pea Soup ("Erwten Soup") 40
Peas Vinaigrette 149
Peach Toast Colvmns 85
Peach Crumble 215
Peanut Soup, Cream of 39
Peanut Brittle 213
Peanut Butter Fudge 213

Pear Salad, Ginger 51
Pear Kuchen 215
PECAN(S)
   Charleston Huguenot Torte 221
   Chicken Pecan Quiche 105
   Chocolate Butternut Sauce 178
   Cranberry Nut Bread 78
   Pecan Cheese Pie 184
Pepper Jelly 173
Pepper Steak 127
Peppery Chicken Crispy 119
Pesto, Chicken 112
Pesto Sauce 173
Pickle Slices, Crispy 168
Pickled Herring 20
Pickled Mushrooms 20
Pickles, Ice Box Cucumber 171
PIE
   Apple Candy Pie 185
   Apple Crumb Pie 185
   Apricot Delight Pie 186
   Banana-Caramel Pie 186
   Banana Split Sundae Pie 187
   Black Walnut Pie 187
   Chocolate Banana Creme Pie 188
   French Silk Pie 189
   Fudge Pie 189
   Grasshopper Pie 181
   Ice Cream Pie 190
   Lemon Cream Pie 190
   Lemon Fluff Pie 182
   Mandarin Orange Pie 190
   Meat/Main Dish
      Down Jersey Clam Pie 92
      Mainstay Chicken Pie 113
      Old Fashioned Chicken Pot Pie 117
   Mocha Angel Pie 181
   Mud Pie 188
   Pecan Cheese Pie 184
   Pie Crust
      Cocount Pie Crust 188
      Flaky Pie Crust 191
   Shoo-Fly Pie 183
   Tom's Rum Cream Pie 183
   Whole Strawberry Pie 184
   Vegetable
      Green Tomato Pie 154
      Zucchini Pie 159
PINEAPPLE
   Baked Pineapple 165
   Grandma Egelhoff's Pineapple
      Salad 51
   Mandarin Orange Pineapple Cake . 191
   Pineapple Pudding 167

Sparkling Apricot Pineapple
   Punch 27
Piroski 22
Plum Jelly, Beach 165
Poached Fish Creole 97
Pop Pancakes 86
Porcupine Meat Balls 127
PORK (Also See Ham)
   Apples 'N Stuffing Pork Chops ... 135
   Loin of Pork Apricot 134
   Mandarin Pork and Vegetables .. 134
   Reuben Meatloaf 128
   Sukiyaki 131
   Sweet and Sour Sauce 135
   Zesty Pork Chops 136
POTATO(ES) (Also See Sweet Potato)
   English Fish and Chips 93
   Green Bean and Potato Salad 45
   Holiday Potato Dish 150
   Make Ahead Mashed Potatoes ... 149
   Mother's Potato Salad 50
   Oven-Crisp Potatoes 152
   Second Time Mashed Potatoes (Potato
      Cakes) 150
   Turnip-Potato Patties 155
POULTRY (See Separate Listings)
Prune Cake, Carrot, Raisin 200
Prune Cake 205
PUDDING
   Bread Pudding with Whiskey
      Sauce 219
   Country Style Corn Pudding 145
   German Pudding Sauce 169
   Hot Fudge Pudding 222
   Huntington Corn Pudding 145
   Mother Willis's Holiday Pudding . 222
   Pineapple Pudding 167
   Pudding Cake, Fudge 194
PUMPKIN
   Pumpkin Bread 80
   Pumpkin Shell Casserole 174
   Pumpkin Soup 40
PUNCH
   Champagne Punch 27
   Florida Sunshine Punch 30
   Mocha Milk Punch 28
   Slush Punch 28
   Sparkling Apricot Pineapple
      Punch 27
   Whiskey Sour Punch 27

Q

Quark 166
Queen Victoria's Coronation Tart .. 182

INDEX

Quiche, Chicken Pecan 105
Quiche, Crab 92
Quick And Easy Banana Bread 77
Quick Chicken Casserole 106
Quick Sour Cream Rolls 81
Quick Whole Wheat Bread 83
Quickie Chicken 116

R
Racked of Lamb Moutarde 133
Raisin, Prune Carrot Cake 200
Ranger Chicken 116
Raspberry Cream in Chicken 121
Raspberry Lemon Ribbion Dessert . 216
Red Chicken Jambalaya 115
Refrigerator Mint Bars 210
Relish, Shoe Peg 175
Reuben Meatloaf 128
Ribbon Oyster Stew 96

RICE
Artichoke Rice Salad 43
Beef in Sherry 128
Crab and Rice Ramekins 90
Green Rice 161
Holiday Cornish Hens 123
Moo Goo Gai Pien 117
One Pan Paella 122
Porcupine Meat Balls 127
Rice Casserole 162
Savannah Red Rice 161
Shrimp Casserole 101
Shrimp Jambalaya 104
Sweet and Sour Pork 135
Rolls, Quick Sour Cream 81

RUM
Rum Balls 208
Rum Cake 204
Rum Slush 31
Tom's Rum Cream Pie 183
Walnut Rum Cake 206
Rye Slice, Party 22

S
SALAD(S)
Congealed
Cucumber Mousse 45
Ginger Pear Salad 51
Grandma Egelhoff's Pineapple Cream
  Salad 51
Lulu Salad 49
Whipped Fruit Salad 55
Fruit
Orange Cream Fruit Salad 50

Meat/Seafood
Baked Chicken Salad 107
Chicken Salad Balls 13
Chicken Salad Habana 48
Christmas Salad 43
Cobb Salad 44
Molded Chicken Salad 49
Overnight Layered Chicken
  Salad 47
Soy Chicken Salad 48
Taco Salad 55
Pasta/Rice
Artichoke Rice Salad 43
Garden Pasta Salad 72
Matchless Macaroni Salad 70
Pasta Salad 72
Vegetable/Tossed Green
Broccoli Salad 46
Cauliflower Salad 47
Green Bean and Potato Salad 45
Hearts of Palm Salad 44
Mother's Potato Salad 50
Overnight Tossed Salad 54
Sauerkraut Salad 52
Slaw (See Separate Listings)
Three Bean Salad 54
SALAD DRESSING
Bacon Scallion Dressing 167
Garlic Mint Dressing 169
Salmon Mold 23
Salmon Mousse 23
Salmon Strudel 98
Sand Tarts, Drop 212
SANDWICHES
Cheese Dreams 56
Ham Bar-B-Q's 57
Hot Ham and Cheese Sandwich ... 56
Inside-Out Sandwiches 57
Kentucky Hot Browns 58
SAUERKRAUT
Alsatin Braised Sauerkraut 141
Reuben Meatloaf 128
Sauerkraut Salad 52
SAUSAGE
"Erwten Soup" 40
One Pan Paella 122
Ranger Chicken 116
Sausage Strata 64
Spaghetti Superb 74
Savannah Red Rice 161
SAUCE(S)
Meat/Seafood
Apple Onion Sauce 165
Chicken Barbecue Sauce 167

Clam Sauce 90
Dill Sauce 169
Jezebel's Sauce 171
Mock Hollandaise Sauce 173
Pesto Sauce 173
Summer's Barbecue Sauce 176
Union League Sauce 177
Pasta
Pesto Sauce 173
Sweet
Chocolate Butternut Sauce 178
Chocolate Mint Sauce 218
German Pudding Sauce 169
Hot Fudge Sauce 170
Lemon Sauce 172
Marshmallow Fudge Sauce 172
Whiskey Sauce 219
Vegetable
Hollandaise Sauce 170
Scallion Dressing, Bacon 167
Scalloped Apples 174
Scalloped Oysters 98
Scallops with Mixed Peppers, Seviche of
Bay 101
Scotch Eggs 67
SEAFOOD (See Individual Seafood
Listings)
Fish Casserole 94
Nassau Seafood Chowder 42
Seafood Brochette 99
Seafood Canapes 24
Seafood Chowder 41
Seafood Newburg 100
Seafood Rarebit Souffle 100
Seafood with Curry Sauce 100
Second Time Mashed Potatoes (or Potato
Cakes) 150
Sesame Chicken, Oven Baked 106
Seviche of Bay Scallops with Mixed
Peppers 101
Shekerlachmasa Cookies 211
SHERRY(IED)
Beef in Sherry 128
Sherried Beef 132
Sherried Ham 136
Sherried Sweet Potato Casserole . 151
Veal with Sherry Cream Sauce .. 138
Shoe Pig Relish 175
Shoo-Fly Pie 183
Short Bread, Canadian 208
Shortcut Monkey Bread 80
SHRIMP
One Pan Paella 122
Shrimp and Artichoke Hearts En

Casserole 102
Shrimp and Cheese Casserole 102
Shrimp Butter 25
Shrimp Casserole 101
Shrimp Casserole Surprise 103
Shrimp Creole 103
Shrimp Dip 24
Shrimp in Herb Butter Sauce 104
Shrimp Jambalaya 104
Sinful Chocolate Dessert 214
SLAW
Cholesterol-Free Cole Slaw 52
Creamy Summer Slaw 53
Sweet and Simple Coleslaw 53
Slush Punch 28
Soda Bread, Irish 81
Souffle, Seafood Rarebit 100
Souffle, Zucchini 159
SOUP
Asparagus Vichyssoise 35
Beef Stock Lentil Soup 39
Celery Soup 35
Chowder (See Separate Listings)
Crab Bisque 36
Cream of Mushroom Soup 36
Cream of Parsnip Soup 39
Cream of Peanut Soup 39
"Erwten Soup" 40
French Onion Soup 37
Hannah's Homemade Soup 37
Pumpkin Soup 40
Vegetable Soup 42
Sour Cream Rolls, Quick 81
Sour Cream Waffles 85
Southern Spoon Bread 82
Soy Chicken Salad 48
SPAGHETTI
Chicken Casserole 112
Easy Turkey Tetrazzini 124
Spaghetti Ala Venita 74
Spaghetti Alla Carbonara 73
Spaghetti Superb 74
Sparkling Apricot Pineapple Punch . 27
Spicy Mayonnaise 175
SPINACH
E-Z Fish Flosentine 94
Flounder in Spinach 95
Geoff and Bobbie's Spinach
Terrific 153
Green Noodles 71
Mushrooms Florentine 148
Spinach and Artichoke Bake 152
Spinach Artichoke Casserole 152
Spinach Casserole 154

INDEX

Veggie Dip 26
Spizzata 137
Spoon Bread, Southern 82
Spring Compote 176
Steak Romano 124
STEW
   Carefree Stew 125
   Hot Dog Stew 137
   Ribbon Oyster Stew 96
Stilton or Blue Cheese Wafers 25
Stir Fry, Vegetable 156
STRATA
   Chicken and Stuffing Strata 108
   Sausage Strata 64
   Vegetable Strata 157
Strawberry Pie, Whole 184
Strudel, Salmon 98
Stuffed Bread 25
Stuffed Mushrooms 19
Sukiyaki 131
Summer's Barbecue Sauce 176
Super Cider Float 32
Swedish Christmas Glogg 31
Sweet and Simple Coleslaw 53
Sweet and Sour Chicken 115
Sweet and Sour Pork 135
Sweet Bell Pepper Jam 176
SWEET POTATO
   Sherried Sweet Potato Casserole . 151
   Sweet Potato Bread 83
   Sweet Potato Muffins 82
Sweet Spicy Chicken Breasts 122
Swiss Cheese Puffs 26
T
Taco Salad 55
Tamale, Chicken 119
Tangy Spread 26
Tart, Queen Victoria's Coronation .. 182
Tarts, Cherry Blossom Cheese 221
Tetrazzini, Easy Turkey 124
Three Bean Salad 54
Three "C" Casserole 114
Toast, Colvmns Peach 85
Toast, French 84
Tomato Pie, Green 154
Tom's Rum Cream Pie 183
Torte, Charleston Huguenot 221
Torte with Coffee Filling Nut 216
Tortilla Surprise, California
   Chicken 107
Tuiles Aux Amandes (Almond
   Cookies) 208
Tuna Scallop 104
TURKEY
   Easy Turkey Tetrazzini 124

Kentucky Hot Browns 58
Turkey Piccata 124
Turnip Roast 155
Turnip-Potato Patties 155
Turnovers, Cherry Cream Cheese .. 220
U
Union League Sauce 177
V
Vanilla Extract 177
Vanilla Wafers, Danish 207
VEAL
   Easy Veal Marsala 137
   Spizzata 137
   Veal Taillevent 138
   Veal with Sherry Cream Sauce .. 138
VEGETABLES (Also See Individual
   Vegetable Listings, Salads- Vegetable/
   Tossed Green and Soups)
   California Vegetable Medley 157
   Mandarin Pork and Vegetables .. 134
   Mixed Vegetable Casserole 156
   Pasta Primavera 73
   Sukiyaki 131
   Vegetable Lasagna 158
   Vegetable Soup 42
   Vegetable Stir Fry 156
   Vegetable Strata 157
   Veggie Dip 26
Vichyssoise, Asparagus 35
Victorian Currant Cakes 201
Vinaigrette 44
Vinaigrette, Peas 149
Virginia Apple Pudding 218
W
Waffles, Sour Cream 85
Walnut Pie, Black 187
Walnut Rum Cake 206
Whipped Cream, Wine 177
Whipped Fruit Salad 55
Whiskey Sauce 219
Whiskey Sour Punch 27
Whole Strawberry Pie 184
Whole Wheat Bread, Quick 83
Windsor Baked Steak 126
Wine Jelly, Cranberry 168
Wine Whipped Cream 177
Yogurt Bread 84
Z
Zesty Pork Chops 136
ZUCCHINI
   California Vegetable Medley 157
   Mashed Potato Zucchini Casserole.. 151
   Zucchini Pie 159
   Zucchini Souffle 159

AN INVITATION TO JOIN THE
MID-ATLANTIC CENTER FOR THE ARTS (MAC)

MAC consists of over 1,100 members who volunteer time or offer support through membership dues.

MAC membership is open to everyone and provides many benfits, including a monthly newsletter, notice of upcoming events, invitations to special receptions and parties, as well as free admission to Physick Estate, Walking and Trolley Tours and reduced admission to Theatre By The Sea, Vintage Films, and other special events.

We welcome you to join our labor of love.

MEMBERSHIP FORM

Type of Membership/Annual Dues:

_____	Student	$5.00
_____	Individual	$20.00
_____	Joint	$25.00
_____	Family	$30.00
_____	Patron	$50.00
_____	Sponsor	$100.00
_____	Business	$100.00

Please make checks payable to MAC, and send too:

MAC
P.O. Box 340
Cape May, N.J. 08204

Name _____

Address _____

_____ Zip _____

Phone _____